Dear Payton,

Hope you enjoy
wrote about the
God's creation.
Wish you God's abundant
blessings!

BOB JOSEPH PULLAMPALLY

The
INVISIBLE THINGS
of GOD

BOB JOSEPH

ISBN 978-1-63903-132-0 (paperback)
ISBN 979-8-88751-483-3 (hardcover)
ISBN 978-1-63903-133-7 (digital)

Christian Faith Publishing
832 Park Avenue
Meadville, PA 16335
www.christianfaithpublishing.com

All quoted verses have been taken from the King James Version of the Holy Bible.

All images used are from public domain and released under Creative Commons license with permission to use without attribution.

Printed in the United States of America

This book is dedicated to my God and my Lord, Jesus Christ, the Creator of the universe, the One Who sustains us and provides for us, the One Who had mercy on me and saved me from the power of darkness and brought me into His marvelous light, that I may know and live for the truth.

CONTENTS

For the <u>invisible</u> things of him from the creation of the world are clearly seen, being understood <u>by the things that are made</u>, even his eternal power and Godhead.

—Romans 1:20

INTRODUCTION

Man has made unbelievable and astounding advancements in science and engineering throughout history. It is no doubt a wonder if we think about the journey we earthly mortals have undertaken throughout the centuries to increase our understanding of our surroundings and use this knowledge and the resources available to us to discover new methods and invent new things to improve our standard of living. Through ongoing research and development and with the help of the industries we have made, we are continually making the daily necessities and activities of our lives easier and quicker. We can do things quicker, better, and easier than ever before!

Take for example our means of communication. We have really come a long way! To communicate, humans once used to rely only on talking face-to-face or sending human messengers to convey information and messages. From there, we slowly advanced to writing and sending messages on stone tablets, scrolls, papyri, paper, and so forth. More recently, we have progressed to communicating through the telephone, telegrams, the modern postal system, newspapers, radios, television, cell phone voice calls, text messages, web pages, emails, video calls, and now even holograms!

Yes, we understand much more about the world we live in today than we ever did. We have used much of this knowledge to our advantage in the fields of engineering, medicine, agriculture, and so on. Yet when we consider what we know about nature today, our ultimate conclusions are vastly different from person to person. The facts are the same, but what we infer from them varies. Nonetheless, what matters is the truth. Truth is independent of opinions. It is worthy of pursuit above all else.

This book is a compilation of some of my own thoughts and insights, particularly at times when I observe and learn about the treasures hidden in nature. Having known God through a personal relationship with Him, I feel great joy in my heart when I realize the depth of what He has done in this world through His work of creation and for me personally. When I look at the beautiful landscapes or travel through the mountains or spend time on a scenic beach or observe the green fields or see a beautiful flower or gaze into the sky on a starry night or learn of the vastness of the universe or understand new concepts in engineering, I cannot refrain from ascribing credit for all this to the God Whom I have known and walk with.

There are a lot of pictures within the pages of this book. I hope that the reader does not simply glance over them. Instead, I encourage you to carefully look at them in detail (if you're curious about what you are looking at, there is a photo index at the end for your reference). My intent is to display and demonstrate, with some examples, the beauty that God has embedded in nature and also share many of the things that personally interest and fascinate me and bring joy to my heart. My hope is that after reading this book, you will approach nature and science with a new perspective. The next time you interact with nature in some form—whether it is through a visit to the park, or a walk in the garden, or by a picture on the wall, or by reading about an interesting creature, or through the study of science and mathematics—my desire is that you will remember the works of the true God and Creator of everything, and your heart will be moved to praise Him.

GOD AND SCIENCE

THE KNOWLEDGE OF GOD

Who is God?
How do we know that God exists?
Does faith in God contradict science?
What do we know about His nature?
How can we know more about Him?
What do we gain from knowing Him?
What do we lose from not knowing Him?

God is invisible. It is true that we cannot directly see Him with our eyes or hear Him with our ears. We are not able to experience Him using any of our physical senses. He is our Creator and the greatest, most important, highest, and most excellent person in the universe. He is present everywhere and sees everyone and everything. Still, our eyes have been denied the capability and privilege of beholding any physical aspect of His form. This makes knowing Him and believing in Him rather difficult for many of us. Difficult, but not impossible.

There have been many people in history who have seen visions of God's image, heard His voice, and seen glimpses of His holiness, greatness, power, and glory. Of course, many people saw Jesus Christ in person while He lived on earth, even after He resurrected from death (with an immortal body). However, no man has seen the Almighty God in the fullness of His glory. Although we are not able to physically see Him directly or hear His audible voice on a daily basis, He still wants us to understand Who He is and many of the mysteries that surround His nature, character, and will.

There are many ways by which we can know and experience the true living God. The most direct way to know *about* God is

3

through the Bible, the inerrant and unchanging Word of God. We can also know about Him through the testimonies and experiences shared by other Christians who know Him. Another way we can know about Him is by observing nature and through the study of science. This may sound odd because science is often presented as a contradiction to the knowledge of God. However, that is not really true. The study of science and nature reveals many things about God. Without any words but with great eloquence, the heavens and all of nature declare the *creativity, greatness, might*, and *wisdom* of God.

We can know *about* God in these ways, but we can only *know Him* and *experience Him* through a personal relationship with Him. As with any human relationship, having knowledge about someone is not the same as knowing him/her personally. For example, an autobiography or a TV documentary may enable us to know many things about a famous leader or someone we admire, but no amount of reading or watching can compare with the experience of knowing them personally. Knowing about God even through the most in-depth theological studies does not benefit us much if we are not able to know Him personally. The wonderful thing about God is that He wants to have an individual, close and personal relationship with each one of us.

If you are *not a Christian*, all this might be a little hard to understand or accept as you start reading this book. Your initial inclination may be to dismiss all this due a presupposition that God does not exist or that Jesus Christ is not the God and Creator of this world and the universe. My hope is that this presupposition does not prevent you from progressing through the pages of this book until the very end. As you do this, I also hope that all preconceived opinions and beliefs give way to a critical, unbiased, and objective analysis of what is presented here, which ultimately leads to a belief in and a loving relationship with the God of the universe. And if you are someone "on the fence" about God and the Bible, I hope that my thoughts that are expressed through this book will serve to push you over to the right side, that is, the side of truth.

So before you begin, I urge you to sincerely consider these questions:

If there really is a God, would you want to know Him?
If this God is as loving as (or more than) what is described in this book, would you want a close relationship with Him?

WHAT IS NATURE SAYING?

So what exactly is nature saying about God? In other words, what are the reasonable conclusions we can draw about God from the facts that we have collected about nature and the mysteries that we have unraveled through our observations and scientific discoveries over the past few thousand years?

The following is a very short summary of the qualities of God that are displayed in nature. It can also be viewed as a summary of what we are going to be looking at in greater detail in the sections that follow.

God's Creativity

The philosophy behind good architecture generally includes three components—form, function, and structure. Like most great architects, along with function and structure, God did not forget to provide form (or beauty) to His creation. The large and small features in His design are not limited to the mere fulfillment of their function or purpose. It becomes clear from the scrutiny of details that many aspects of His design are purely for aesthetic purposes. It is also noteworthy that the only part of His creation that can acknowledge and appreciate this beauty in God's created world—whether it is in a small scale or large—is mankind.

It may then be reasonable to conclude that God has made this earth beautiful primarily for us.

God's Strength and Might

Surely it is not such a far-fetched notion that the Creator is greater than the creation. The vastness of the universe, the size of the objects that it contains, and the great amounts of energy hidden in the things that God has made all provide a glimpse of how great and powerful He is and how small we are in comparison. At a closer level, the uncontrollable forces of nature that are now increasingly frequent show glimpses of His power, our own helpless frame in comparison, as well as the consequences of His wrath and the severity of His judgment.

God's Ingenuity

The complexity of the created world and the engineering perfection inherent in the things that are made reveal that God is wiser beyond our knowledge or imagination. We can appreciate this better when we compare His created work to things that we know to be complex in our world, particularly man-made products and systems like electronics, computers, aircrafts, chemical processing plants, and the like.

God's Love

God's faithful provisions that sustain our lives on earth—sunshine, rain, and food—show His constant care and compassion for all of mankind. Above all these, having a personal relationship with God will reveal to us many other aspects of His character such as His abundant love, mercy, and goodness.

So let us look at all these qualities of God in the sections that follow and understand how the natural world reveals these things about God.

"For by him were all things created, that are in heaven, and that are in earth, visible and invisible, whether they be thrones, or dominions, or principalities, or powers: all things were created by him, and for him: And he is before all things, and by him all things consist" (Colossians 1:15–16).

BEAUTY IN CREATION

NATURAL BEAUTY

It is not a little-known fact that God has made this earth and everything in it beautiful. Throughout the ages, man has found inspiration, peace, and joy from beholding and experiencing the beauty of God's creation. So even today, beautiful scenes from nature please our eyes and fill our hearts with amazement and delight.

We are filled with joy when we come across natural scenes like a field (or even a small garden) of colorful flowers, a rainbow in the sky, grand snow-covered mountain ranges, a thick blanket of white fluffy clouds from the window of an airplane, falling water, sunrise and sunset, a flock of sheep grazing on a green field, the multicolored trees of autumn against the backdrop of the bright blue sky with a few scattered bright white clouds, a flowing stream of clear water among the rocks, a tropical beach with white sand and clear, shallow water, water lilies in a pond, a still blue lake that reflects the sky, or the sky on a starry, moonlit night (you can probably tell, I've described my own natural delights!).

Modern technology has allowed us to see these things virtually. Yet the virtual experience is nothing compared to that of physically enjoying the beauty of God's created world. Isn't that why we travel long distances (especially with the ones we love) and spend time, money, and effort to visit and experience some of this natural beauty? Sometimes, some of the emotions that flood our hearts when we see such things are indescribable and inexpressible. Still, we love to share what we feel and experience with others. So we capture it on our cameras or cell phones to share it with our friends and loved ones.

We try to make these natural scenes a part of our daily lives by bringing them into our living and working environments mainly because of the pleasing effect they provide. This is probably why we have waterfalls and fountains beside or inside our buildings. We fill our walls, phones, cameras, postcards, souvenirs, and computer desktop backgrounds with scenes from nature. We decorate our homes, gardens, and office desks with beautiful flowers and plants. We do these things because of the beauty and color these natural scenes and flowers add to our lives. Can we deny that God's earth is beautiful?

The beautiful colors
on this Gouldian finch
represent one of God's
diverse design features
in His creatures.

DIVERSITY IN DESIGN

When we dive deeper into the *details* of the design of living things, we see that God has not made their appearance plain and boring. He has added a lot of *diversity* in nature by embedding various special aspects into His design. We can see this diversity in all species, whether it be animals, birds, bugs, or plants. The beauty in their creation is characterized by a combination of many features such as colors, patterns, shapes, texture, proportion, symmetry, size, and so forth. For example, all frogs do not look the same. God has created so many types of frogs! Slimy as they are, some of them are really beautiful to look at.

Now, these diverse features can be seen at all scales in nature. They are not only seen in individual plants, flowers, animals, or just living things but also in fields, forests, mountains, landscapes, and even in outer space. Jupiter does not just appear as a plain gray piece of round rock, but it looks rather nice with its pattern of stripes and shades (apparently due to the gases in its atmosphere). God may have done it this way probably so that man can look at these and marvel and know God. Or else, He may have done it simply for the pleasure and enjoyment it brings us.

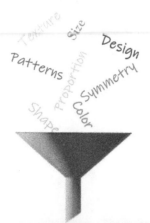

Texture Size Design
Patterns Proportion Symmetry
Shape Color

So it is interesting to look closely into the design of created things and appreciate the obvious beauty that we may easily miss amidst the din and bustle of our fast-paced lives. Then we can see that God's close attention to detail is remarkable and quite evident in all the things that He has made, for example, the pattern displayed on a bug, or the way a blooming flower appears, or the color of a fungus (mushroom), or the well-crafted shape, symmetry, colors, and pattern of a butterfly's wings or that of a peacock's beautiful tail feathers, or the design of a deer's antlers, or the fractal structure of a snowflake, or even the beautiful construction and colors of our eyes.

When we buy something for ourselves, we are very much particular about how things *look* and not just what they do. If not, we would all be wearing clothes or driving cars that look the same! So in general, when man makes something (like clothes, cars, homes, buildings, etc.), he does not just design it and make it solely to meet its functional need. We care quite a lot about the appearance of things. God has done something similar in nature with all its visual diversity. Although some of the patterns, colors, and external design features are functional in nature, most of them serve no other purpose than to add beauty and diversity. So whether the creature's size is small…

...medium...

18

...or large, this diversity in the external appearances of
God's created beings is noteworthy and fascinating.

C LORS

Of all the external features that God has embedded in the natural world, the most outstanding one that contributes greatly to the splendor of His created work is the diversity in colors that is seen all around. All of creation is filled with vibrant colors that please our eyes. It appears that God has painted this world with His multicolored paint brush! Thus, it is no wonder that colorful natural scenes have been depicted in many of our paintings. So in all components of His creation like fishes, fruits, flowers, vegetables, birds, bugs, animals, or landscapes, there are so many shades and colors for us to look at and appreciate.

The aurora borealis (or northern/polar lights) is a colorful display of lights seen close to the polar regions.

The peacock has a beautiful crown on its head, a bright-blue color on its neck, and a beautiful pattern on its long flowy tail feathers—truly a majestic display of beauty in the animal kingdom. The next few pages display some more examples of colorful birds.

The blue jay's wings and
tail have beautiful blue
and white pattern.

Have you ever seen a bird with blue feet? Meet the blue-footed booby. On your right, you can see a small variety of birds that represent the colorful diversity in God's creation. The toucan and magpie are my personal favorites!

FLOWERS

When describing beauty in nature or the variety of colors in God's design, it would be inappropriate to leave out a section dedicated to flowers. Other than attracting pollinators to their sweet nectar, these beauties silently offer so much color and life to our daily activities. Whether it is at a restaurant table; at a wedding ceremony; in a bride's hand, hair, or car; at a funeral; in our gardens; flower beds; or living rooms, we have accepted these delicate but attractive natural ornaments manufactured by God as worthy decorations.

Some of us toil in planting, watering, and nurturing them. This is not for any fruit that we expect them to bear for us but simply for the beauty they add to our homes. God has given us these natural ornaments to adorn our rooms, houses, buildings, and functions, and we use them with various mix-and-match configurations according to our personal preference and artistic taste.

Not only do these flowers provide visual delight due to their different shapes, sizes, patterns, and colors; but many of them also please our hearts with their sweet fragrance. My personal favorite is the smell of jasmine. Even many of the artificial scents that we produce (like air fresheners, soaps, perfumes, etc.) try to resemble or remind us of these natural fragrances. Sometimes we put them in bowls or bags and use them even after they've died and dried!

These flowers also serve as a means to silently express ourselves on many occasions. Without any words, they help us to convey our love to a dear one, to honor an important guest at a function, to express our care and sentiments during a hospital visit or to display our gratitude and love when visiting a friend. They are always welcomed as worthy gifts even though they are relatively inexpensive. No doubt, they are symbols of good, and so we use them to express the good thoughts and intentions of our hearts. Thank God for flowers!

Now we may be able to make these flowers from plastic; but there is no material on earth that can replicate or substitute the texture, smoothness, and feel of a flower petal on our fingers.

These beauties are so much more elegant than any of us in our finest attire. Even the wildflowers that spread themselves by the sides of the roads and highways or the white daisies and purple asters that grow on their own in our backyards are so beautiful. They may not be deliberately planted by us, but they spark in us a sort of admiration. Some of us may even gather these daisies and asters and place them in our homes in vases (I won't deny doing such things).

As Jesus Christ said, the lilies of the field are arrayed in a grander manner than King Solomon ever was in all his majesty and pomp. And truly this is the work of God!

"And why take ye thought for raiment? Consider the lilies of the field, how they grow, they toil not, neither do they spin: And yet I say unto you, That even Solomon in all his glory was not arrayed like one of these" (Matthew 6:28–29).

MUSIC

We have been looking at the beauty in nature that we can *see*. Beauty does not necessarily have to be restricted to things that please our visual senses. Music is a beautiful part of God's creation that pleases our ears although it does not offer anything for our eyes. We clap our hands, tap our feet, snap our fingers, sway our bodies, and shake our heads in enjoyment and appreciation of the pleasure that it provides.

Even from ancient times, man has been drawn to the pleasing, soothing, attractive effects of music. It seems that the ways that the basic seven notes (do-re-mi-fa-sol-la-ti) can be combined to make pleasing sounds are just endless! That is why people have been composing music for ages. The laws that govern music (scale, pitch, rhythm, chords, measure, notes, etc.) ensure that there is structure and repeatability. We use these laws to compose songs and music that sound pleasant and not just random noise. These laws and the underlying foundational principles (like the sounds produced by each instrument and the frequencies it generates) were all designed and established in nature by God. So music itself is a reflection of God's creativity! So we sing and make melody in our hearts to praise Him for all His wonderful works.

"I will sing of the mercies of the LORD for ever: with my mouth will I make known thy faithfulness to all generations" (Psalms 89:1).

OTHER SENSES

So far, we have *mainly* discussed natural beauty related to our two senses—seeing and hearing (although we touched very briefly on other things like texture and fragrance). The point here is that God has deliberately embedded in His design of the natural world many things that are appealing to each of our senses.

Take for example the food that we eat. We consume food for our body's nutrition. But we often choose what to eat based on how it tastes! So when we eat or drink, it is not just a need we are fulfilling. Food delights and satisfies our hearts because of the way it smells and tastes. If all food looked, smelled, and tasted the same, eating would be a mundane task (like taking a pill daily). Ask a person who has temporarily lost their sense of smell and taste due to illness. They find eating to be a difficult chore! God provided a wide variety of food options for us in nature that allow nourishment and growth for the body and pleasure for the mind. So our celebrations, appreciation, fellowship, and family gatherings usually involve a variety of food and drinks that not only fill our stomachs but also our hearts.

In the same way, God's beauty in the natural world can also be seen in things related to other senses like smell and touch. The inviting smell of fresh grapes, apples, or mangoes have the power to lure us to a fruit stall for a quick drink on a hot day. Many of us find the smell of tulsi leaves, a blooming tree, fresh rain, flowers, and many other natural things to be very pleasing. The feel and touch of a baby's soft skin or a dog's fur appeal to our sense of touch as well!

The Carolina wood duck with all sorts of colors and patterns in its design.

WHAT CAN WE INFER?

So what shall we conclude? What do these observations of diversity in design and the beauty spread out in creation imply? Seeing all this, can a rational mind deny God's deliberate hand in it? Leaving aside all bias and prejudice and seeing the obvious, purposeful, tasteful, and artful details and the creativity in creation, would it not be well fitting for a logically inclined mind to acknowledge, appreciate, and appropriately attribute adoration to God's masterpiece that is the universe?

We know that man's artistic talents and creativity are greatly admired and appreciated. We have museums that display the artwork of talented artists and sculptors. Good works of art are so expensive. Some are even worth millions. Indeed, as a work of art describes the skill and mind of the painter, as a sculpture portrays the talent of the sculptor, as a piece of furniture displays the craftsmanship of the carpenter, as a building or a structure glorifies the architect, the beauty of this world and everything in it and beyond it continue to ever speak throughout all generations about the God Who designed it and created it by His word of power.

Did you know that a tiger's stripe pattern is unique for each individual, just like human fingerprints? Also, the tiger not only has stripes on its outer fur but also on its skin!

GOD'S POWER AND GREATNESS

"For the LORD your God is God of gods, and Lord of lords, a great God, a mighty, and a terrible, which regardeth not persons, nor taketh reward" (Deuteronomy 10:17).

A GREAT GOD

How great is God? How powerful is He? What can His strength be compared to? How can we gauge it, or what can we assume it to be like? We may have heard of Him, but what in this world can we see in order to gain understanding of His greatness, strength, and power?

It is not common or easy for us to see the great power of God by a personal encounter with Him. We would most certainly be overcome by great fear or even consumed if such a thing were to happen. However, He has hidden revelations of His power and greatness in the things that He made such that those of us who care to examine closer and understand can get a glimpse of it.

"Bless the LORD, O my soul, O LORD my God, thou art very great; thou art clothed with honour and majesty. Who coverest thyself with light as with a garment: who stretchest out the heavens like a curtain" (Psalms 104:1–2).

FORCES OF NATURE

Man certainly has had many accomplishments to boast about throughout history. The advancements we have made in the fields of engineering and technology, medicine, manufacturing, arts, politics, and others are significant and certainly commendable. We are also continuously improving in these fields through research and development. When we think about the homes, buildings, industries, roadways, bridges, tunnels, and modes of transportation and communication we have today, we can say that we have indeed come a long way.

One of our most significant achievements is that we have been largely successful in harnessing the many forms of energy found in nature for our use and advantage. This does not mean, however, that we have fully tamed or subdued all the forces of nature. What happens when lightning strikes or when we hear the sound of loud thunder? Are we not reminded of the tremendous amount of energy and power in nature? When we read and hear about earthquakes, floods, hurricanes, tornadoes, avalanches, blizzards, wildfires, volcanic eruptions, and tsunamis, what is our state of mind? Despite all the achievements we have to boast about, do we not get a glimpse

of our own frailty and helplessness? We are unable to prevent or completely withstand any of these natural calamities with any of our own strength or with anything that we have built. Those who have the misfortune of facing any of these can only take cover or try and recover from the damages left behind.

These natural forces are all, in fact, glimpses of the great power of God. As abundantly merciful as He is, we must not forget that He is the Creator of all small and great things in the universe. Every form of energy (wind, electrical, nuclear, chemical, fire, and so on) is subject to His command, and He rules over all. When we see manifestations of these forms of energy in uncontrolled ways, we get an opportunity to think about our smallness and God's greatness. So the theme throughout this section is that if the created things are so great, powerful, vast, large, and so forth, how much more the Creator!

"At this also my heart trembleth, and is moved out of his place. Hear attentively the noise of his voice, and the sound that goeth out of his mouth. He directeth it under the whole heaven, and his lightning unto the ends of the earth. After it a voice roareth: he thundereth with the voice of his excellency; and he will not stay them when his voice is heard. God thundereth marvellously with his voice; great things doeth he, which we cannot comprehend. For he saith to the snow, Be thou on the earth; likewise to the small rain, and to the great rain of his strength" (Job 37:1–6).

"He hath made the earth by his power, he hath established the world by his wisdom, and hath stretched out the heaven by his understanding"
(Jeremiah 51:15).

THE UNIVERSE

Look up!

The sky, the stars, the sun, and the moon have something to say.

"The heavens declare the glory of God; and the firmament sheweth his handywork. Day unto day uttereth speech, and night unto night sheweth knowledge. There is no speech nor language, where their voice is not heard. Their line is gone out through all the earth, and their words to the end of the world" (Psalms 19:1–4).

The sky and everything above it proclaim the glory and greatness of the God Who created everything. They have no words, but all day long they are continually making a very loud statement...just by being there. Language is not a barrier. This statement can be heard all around the world no matter what language you speak. It's just that our ears (hearts, really) need to be tuned appropriately to hear what they are saying.

The little spirals in this picture represent galaxies.
Unfathomable—that's one word
that can be used to describe
the size and expanse of this
universe...and the greatness
of the God, Who created it!

The universe is unimaginably vast. We still do not have an understanding about its boundaries. No one has found the edge of the universe yet. Neither has anyone invented a machine or device that can go there. Its limits stretch out into infinity. Now we may know a lot of facts and figures about the universe and its contents, but when we really think about it, our limited understanding is perhaps unable to actually fathom its physical enormity. Nonetheless, the facts and figures can help a little bit.

Astronomers estimate that there are more than one hundred billion galaxies in the observable universe.[1] We do not have any good estimates on that part of the universe that we are not able to see with existing technology. Just as a quick reminder—one billion is a thousand millions (1×10^9). One million is a thousand thousands. It is also estimated that there are around seventy billion trillion (7×10^{22}) stars in the observable universe.[2] What this implies regarding the greatness of the God Who made all this is really significant. But the physical reality of this is a little hard to digest. So to understand this a little better, let's walk through this information slowly.

Little People in a Big World

To understand our individual significance (mainly from a social standpoint) on this great, big earth we live in, let's first consider the population we live among. Let's start with the city we live in. There are perhaps hundreds of thousands or maybe a few million that inhabit our city. With the hustle and bustle of a normal day, it is easy to be lost in the crowd being just one among these millions struggling to get through another day to meet our dreams and goals, whether they be for prosperity or just survival. Size-wise and significance-wise, we are hardly recognizable in our own cities other than by our friends and family (unless you are a celebrity of some sort).

If we zoom out a little, the picture gets only worse, not any better (i.e., as far as our significance is concerned). In our state and our country, our individual characters, skills, backgrounds, or opinions do not have much significance. A select few may manage to achieve fame and popularity, but generally speaking, the ordinary man is just ordinary and insignificant among the several millions. My point here is not to paint a depressing picture of oneself but only to point out the vastness of the earth that we live in.

So the continent that we dwell in or this large and populous world with more than seven billion people is like an ocean in which we are like droplets. Now, let's look at the earth from a slightly different perspective, that is, from a physical standpoint.

It is fascinating to gaze out of the window of an airplane, especially right before landing or just after taking off from the ground. As we start climbing higher and higher, we see things starting to look different. Soaring at only a few thousand feet, all signs of life on the earth beneath disappear. The people and animals dissolve into the background. The houses and cars turn into miniature toys. We cannot distinguish a Toyota from an Audi, a sedan from an SUV, or a two-bedroom house from a five. The swimming pools are just patches of blue, the stadiums look like cereal bowls, the skyscrapers seem like Lego towers, the large fields of crops look like carpets with different shades of green, and the ships in the ocean (that appear very huge while standing beside them) look like toy boats. I remember flying past the Burj Khalifa in Dubai many times. Even though it is currently the tallest building man has ever built, it is so small even at five or six thousand feet in the air! The point is that as we look at ourselves from a "big picture" perspective through the window of an airplane, it becomes apparent that we (and our things) are quite small in size on this earth!

"It is he that sitteth upon the circle of the earth, and the inhabitants thereof are as grasshoppers; that stretcheth out the heavens as a curtain, and spreadeth them out as a tent to dwell in" (Isaiah 40:22).

The Earth

So this earth that we live in is rather huge in size! The earth has a mean radius of 6,378 kilometers.[3] It contains seven continents that hold the billions of people that inhabit it, along with their homes, roads, buildings, and so on. It also holds five large oceans, several seas and lakes, many rivers, a million mountains, several huge deserts, and millions of square miles of thick forests. In a lifetime, an adventurous explorer may see with his own eyes perhaps a relatively minor portion of this earth. Needless to say, those who are not inclined to an exploratory lifestyle may only get to see a smaller portion of this large earth within their lifetime, especially in this technologically advanced age in which we are mostly restricted by work and not very interested in nature. There are, in fact, so many parts of the earth that man has not even reached or explored, particularly the depths of the oceans (most of the earth's oceans are unexplored due to our limitations).

Now, placing our individual sizes in comparison with the size of the earth and the great big things it contains, few would oppose the suggestion that the earth is very large in size and we are rather tiny. Furthermore, it should not be a surprising concept for a reasonable thinker that the creation is lesser than the Creator. So just by considering the size of the earth alone, an understanding about the greatness of God, its Creator, should begin to develop in our minds.

"I am he; I am the first, I also am the last. Mine hand also hath laid the foundation of the earth, and my right hand hath spanned the heavens: when I call unto them, they stand up together"
(Isaiah 48:12–13).

The Solar System

"He stretcheth out the north over the empty place, and hangeth the earth upon nothing" (Job 26:7).

The earth is part of a system of planets that revolve around the sun in their assigned orbits. It essentially "hangs" with all the other seven planets in the solar system, being held by gravitational forces. To put things in size-wise perspective, the earth is only the fifth largest planet in the solar system. The largest planet is Jupiter, which has a diameter about 11.2 times that of the earth. Its mass is about 2.5 times that of all the other planets combined![4]

Now we are slowly stepping out into the unfathomable realm of scale as far as our limited minds are concerned. In other words, although we know the numbers and figures, we are slowly losing the ability to gauge with our minds what that really means. In the same way, unfathomable is the personality and greatness of Jesus Christ, the One Who created all this.

Jupiter, the largest planet in the solar system, has a diameter about 11.2 times that of the Earth.

Solar flares as high as 100,000 km (more than ten times the diameter of the Earth) can be observed on the surface of the sun.[5]

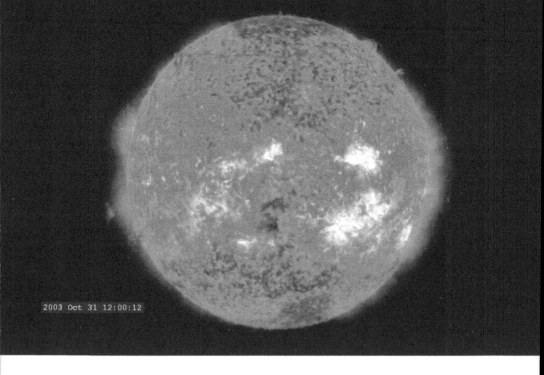

2003 Oct 31 12:00:12

The Sun

The sun is like a great, big ball of fire! It is much larger than all the planets. Its diameter is about 109 times and mass is about 333,000 times that of the earth's.[6] It is large enough to contain about 1.3 million earths inside it![7] The sun puts out so much energy all the time mainly in the form of heat and light. The temperature on the surface of the sun is about 10,000 degrees Fahrenheit![8] This energy is said to be generated by nuclear fusion reactions occurring continuously within the sun. It is unmatched anywhere on earth and is sufficient to consume everything on earth. In fact, even looking directly at the sun can cause eye damage.

The distance of the earth from the sun is found to be optimum. This means that if the earth were closer to the sun or farther away from it, it would not have been habitable. No living creatures or plants would have been able to survive on earth. Yet we are able to use this energy from the sun to our advantage. The size of the sun and the energy it puts out are among the many proclamations made by nature on Who the Almighty God is. The truth of the matter is that even the sun is but a tiny object compared to Who He is.

God asks Job the following questions regarding constellations and His creative work in Job 38:31–32: "Canst thou bind the sweet influences of Pleiades, or loose the bands of Orion? Canst thou bring forth Mazzaroth in his season? Or canst thou guide Arcturus with his sons?"

Stars

The stars that we see in the night sky are also like the sun. However, they are much farther away, and some are much, much bigger. The largest known star is the UY Scuti. Its radius is thought to be about 1,708 times that of the sun[9] (2.4 billion kilometers). Although not as big, there are many such stars in the universe—about seventy billion trillion of them! Now that's a number beyond what our minds can handle! The sun is awe-inspiring by itself with its great size and all the energy and light associated with it. These stars are physically very large objects, and they represent a great amount of energy that is beyond human comprehension. Again, the number of stars and their individual enormity convey an important message about God, their Creator. Since the Creator is obviously always greater than the creation, we can surely conclude that God's strength is truly unmeasurable and infinite.

Yet this great and mighty Creator of all the seventy billion trillion gigantic stars thinks about us and cares for us. He provides for all our needs and takes interest in our well-being. He knows our thoughts and listens to our prayers. He assures us of His love, stills our hearts, and calms our fears.

"When I consider thy heavens, the work of thy fingers, the moon and the stars, which thou hast ordained; What is man, that thou art mindful of him? And the son of man, that thou visitest him?" (Psalms 8:3–4)

Andromeda—the galaxy closest to the Milky Way.

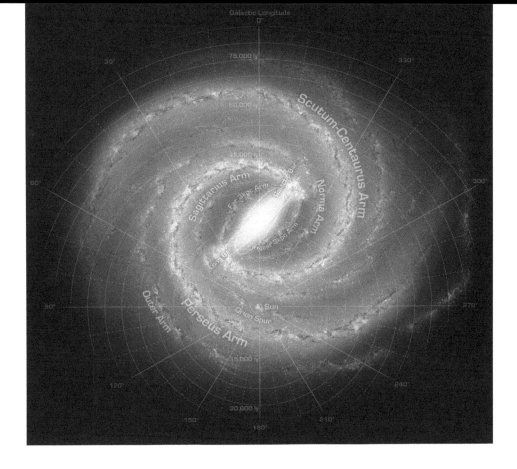

Galaxies

The earth, the sun, and the solar system are part of the Milky Way galaxy (represented above). This is a spiral galaxy that has between one hundred and four hundred billion stars.[10] Proxima Centauri is the nearest star to the sun in the Milky Way. The Milky Way has many spiral arms. The solar system, including the sun and the earth, is believed to be in the Orion arm of the Milky Way. The closest spiral galaxy to ours is called Andromeda (pictured left). The largest known spiral galaxy in the universe is NGC 6872,[11] which is thought to be about five times the size of the Milky Way. There are *billions* of such galaxies in the universe. If we cannot even contain the enormity of the Milky Way in our minds, think about how huge billions of such galaxies would be. Again, these are numbers we know, but what this exactly means surpasses our limited understanding. The universe is huge, much, much beyond our imagination!

*"O LORD our Lord, how excellent is thy name in all the
earth! who hast set thy glory above the heavens"
(Psalms 8:1).*

What Does the Universe Tell Us?

We have not explored or studied the entire universe. What we know today is based on what we are capable of understanding with the technology we have. We do not know what we will find in the coming years. However, one thing we can conclude is that God, Who created all this, is greater than everything that He has created—things both known to us and unknown.

Our understanding of the universe has been changing over time, but the universe itself has not changed along with this. And God has not changed. Even when we did not know as much as we do today about the great and small things in the universe, it was always there.

And God has always been the Almighty, Omnipotent, and Omniscient God Who inhabits eternity.

To Him we owe our devotion for this one reason—He is God.

"Who is the blessed and only Potentate, the King of kings, and Lord of lords; Who only hath immortality, dwelling in the light which no man can approach unto; whom no man hath seen, nor can see: to whom be honour and power everlasting. Amen" (1 Timothy 6:14–16).

The energy stored in the smallest unit of
God's creation (the nucleus of an atom)
is displayed in this massive explosion!

God's Power in Small Things

The previous discussion in this section was mainly aimed at illustrating the greatness of God through an understanding of the physical size of His creation—the universe. Yet His great might and enormous power are also displayed marvelously through the smaller things we encounter on earth. Take electricity for instance. An electrical arc flash (which is a kind of electrical explosion) can get as hot as 35,000 degrees Fahrenheit (hotter than the surface of the sun)! Similarly, even the tiniest of components of the things He has made demonstrate God's amazing power.

All things in the physical world are broadly said to be comprised of matter. One of the smallest known components of all matter is known as the *atom*. The atom is further comprised of subatomic particles, namely electrons, protons, and neutrons. Protons and neutrons are held closely together by a very strong attractive force in the nucleus of the atom. There is a release of an enormous amount of energy when we split the nucleus of an atom. This process is called *nuclear fission*. Man has tried and has been successful in harnessing and using the energy released from nuclear fission for purposes useful to his daily activities. For example, controlled nuclear fission reactions of radioactive isotopes are used to generate electricity. It is also true and quite unfortunate that the energy released from the splitting of atoms has been used by man for mass destruction (the atomic bomb).

The atom, the *smallest* part of God's creation (which is not even visible to man's eye), hides so much of power and energy within it! Imagine how physically powerful God really is!

KNOWLEDGE

It has been said that knowledge is power. However, man is very limited in knowledge. This is probably why we get very excited when we discover something or reach a new milestone in our journey toward exploring the world and the universe we live in. We have many constraints that prevent us from attaining knowledge easily—like distance, time, limitations of our senses (i.e., what we can see, hear, smell, etc.), and limitations in the capacity of our minds.

For example, we cannot at present know everything that is happening in every corner of the world because we cannot be at every place at the same time. In fact, we are mostly unaware of what is happening even in the next room in our own house. We are also not very good at managing more than one thing at a time. For example, we can only perform one task (or maybe two) at a time or listen and

respond to one conversation at a time. We also cannot know everything that happened in history. We have records of some things but not everything.

We cannot see with unaided eyes the things that are very far away like the distant galaxies and stars even though they are extremely large. Neither can we see with our naked eyes things that are very near but extremely small in size like cells, microorganisms, molecules, atoms, subatomic particles, and so forth. We can see light only within a limited range of wavelengths (violet to red). Waves beyond this range (i.e., ultraviolet, infrared) are visible to some creatures in nature but not to humans. Even with the help of technology, we are still unable to see everything in the created universe, far and near. We are only still slowly discovering the secrets of the universe (new stars, new planets, new elements, new species of plants and animals, new properties of materials, new places on earth, etc.). In the same way, we cannot hear everything. Our ears are limited to a certain range of audible frequencies. However, we now have instruments that can help us listen to things we could not hear earlier (e.g., whales communicating). Who knows what sounds that surround our physical environment we are yet to discover!

We are also limited in our understanding of each other. We cannot know the thoughts or motives of another person's heart unless it is revealed to us by their words or actions. Even our closest and most loved ones have thoughts and intents that we cannot know. We are also restricted from understanding events in the spiritual realm like seeing the state of the spirit of a man or seeing angels or recognizing the activities of the devil. We do not have a picture of heaven or hell other than what is revealed in the Bible. However, when we reach our eternal abode with God, we will be able to see things much clearer and understand many truths hidden to us now.

"For now we see through a glass, darkly; but then face to face: now I know in part; but then shall I know even as also I am known" (1 Corinthians 13:12).

Greatness is not just defined by strength or physical power. These limitations in man's knowledge have been described here to accentuate God's greatness displayed by His knowledge. God is omniscient (all-knowing). There are more than seven billion people on the earth at present. God knows every single person individually even to the minutest details of their lives from the time they were conceived to their last breath and even beyond. He simultaneously knows the thoughts of each person, listens to them when (or if) they pray, and responds as appropriate. He provides for all those who trust in Him (and even for those who do not). He watches over them and leads them. He knows the past, the present, and the future of each person and the entire world from the time of creation to eternity. He knows the details of every single event that happened in history, even things that were not recorded in books or passed on through generations.

All the objects in the universe are clearly visible to Him with equal resolution and perfect clarity—from the largest of stars to the smallest subatomic particle. He knows every nook and corner of the universe even up to the uttermost point in His creation. He knows the molecular structure and the chemical and physical properties of all elements (even the ones we have not yet discovered). He knows the state of each of the cells, tissues, muscles, bones, and organs in the bodies of all 7.9 billion people in the world all at once. He knows the detailed geographical structure and terrain on even the smallest asteroid in the farthest galaxy. He knows the chemistry and kinetics of every reaction in the universe. He knows the interactions between every created thing and the way everything in the universe works. He knows everything about everyone and everything everywhere.

God also sees the things we cannot see with our eyes in the spiritual world. Heaven is His throne, and the earth is His footstool (Isaiah 66:1). The angels are His messengers and ministering spirits, and He knows the way and state of the spirits of all men and women. With Him, there is never any misunderstanding. God's knowledge speaks of His greatness!

TIME

The concept in the previous section can also be extrapolated to be applied to another dimension that our world is defined by—time. For convenience, man has divided time into measurable segments like years, months, weeks, days, hours, minutes, seconds, and so on. These measures are linked to the spin and revolution of the earth around its own axis and around the sun.

Now here's a question—if the earth stopped spinning, would time stop? Here are a few more questions that may help with the answer: Would our lives then come to a halt? Would we stop aging? There was an incident during the time of Joshua during which he commanded the sun and moon to stand still for an entire day (you can read about it in the book of *Joshua chapter 10*). What do you think happened to time then? Also, there was an incident in which the Prophet Isaiah gave a sign to King Hezekiah for the healing he would receive from God for a deadly disease he had. He said that the shadow on the sundial of Ahaz would go ten degrees backward. So the sun went ten degrees backward on the sundial (Isaiah 38:7). What do you think happened to time here? Did time go backward when the sun's position went backward? Perhaps, based on the obvious answers to these questions, we can infer that time is not *defined* by the earth, sun, or moon, or by our clocks but only *measured* by them.

As humans, we are physically constrained by how much we can subdivide time. For example, events that happen in milliseconds, microseconds, or nanoseconds cannot be traced by our eyes or processed by our minds quick enough. Nonetheless, we have successfully developed technology that can slow things down (in the virtual world, not physical) to help us see these events and measure the time they take. We can also speed up things that are too slow for us to stay on and observe. We use time-lapse videos to watch really slow things like the germination and growth of a seed into a plant, the movement of clouds, the view of the Milky Way shifting with the revolution of the earth, and the like.

We can store memories of past events in our minds and record them as videos, but we have not developed (nor can we ever develop) technology to view the future. We are very limited with respect to time. Our life itself is limited to a certain period of time. We are born at a certain time. We live for a certain duration and will die at a specific time. No matter what we do, we cannot defy this limitation. Neither can we go back in time to a period before we were born, nor can we extend our lives beyond a certain period.

God, however, is not constrained by time. His greatness is highlighted in His supremacy over time. The events that happen in milliseconds or over millennia are known to Him with equal clarity. His realm and domain exist outside the constraints of time, and so He knows the past, present, and future with absolute certainty.

"For a thousand years in thy sight are but as yesterday when it is past, and as a watch in the night" (Psalms 90:4).

*"*LORD*, thou hast been our dwelling place in all generations. Before the mountains were brought forth, or ever thou hadst formed the earth and the world, even from everlasting to everlasting, thou art God"* (Psalms 90:1–2).

MIRACLES

Miracles reveal God's greatness. A miracle can be described as an unusual or wondrous event that is often beyond expectations or explanation and sometimes defies the laws of nature. Some events that are part of our everyday life can still be considered miracles just because they are inexplicable or just simply amazing. For example, the way or fact that a seed sown in the soil shoots up to be a new plant is an everyday miracle that goes unnoticed. Another one is how a yolk-filled egg that we eat for breakfast can turn into a living creature given the right incubating environment. The egg is so perfectly designed to provide air and nutrition to the growing embryo inside it. The metamorphosis process through which a caterpillar turns into a pupa that, through a mysterious process inside the cocoon, turns into a beautiful butterfly is another amazing everyday process. The biggest everyday miracle to me is how one single embryo divides itself (externally unaided) into cells, tissues, and organs that have specific form and function and finally becomes a living, functional, breathing person with a mind, body, and spirit! This process is repeated countless times among the billions in the world and yields similar results every time.

Other than these everyday miracles that are part of the natural world, God performs specific circumstance-based miracles also. When Jesus Christ was on earth, He visibly performed many law-of-nature-defying miracles that were witnessed by many people. He walked on water; calmed the storms; fed thousands with just a few pieces of bread and fishes; turned water to wine; healed the blind, lame, deaf and dumb; cast out evil spirits; and even raised people from the dead. He Himself also was resurrected from the dead with an immortal and incorruptible body and ascended to heaven. These were all recorded in the four gospel books in the Bible. In addition to these, His disciples performed many similar miracles including healing and bringing the dead back to life. Even today, anyone who lives in close communion with Jesus Christ will testify of the many miracles they witness in their lives like His divine provision in impossible circumstances, healing from diseases, and deliverance from the bondage of sin. Every time these happen, the beneficiary realizes God's greatness in defying circumstances and expected outcomes along with His care for us.

The LORD hath been mindful of us: he will bless us (Psalms 115:12).

LOVE, GOODNESS, AND MERCY

God's strength, power, and authority are not the only things that highlight His greatness. God is superior to all creation in goodness. There is no one better than Him in character or any quality that is good. He is supremely holy, just, perfect, and righteous. The extent of God's goodness, love, and mercy displays His greatness.

Humans are rather poor in these areas in our natural state (but we can be enriched in these qualities as we are transformed into the image and nature of Christ through our relationship with Him). Our good qualities like love, mercy, kindness, goodness, and the like have so many limitations. Purposely or not, knowingly or unknowingly, we lay down so many conditions and boundaries for us to love others. We can quite easily love those who love us back, those who meet our expectations, those who are good to us, those who value us, those who respect us, those who listen to us, those who help us, those who have interests and character similar to ours, those who we can get along with easily, those who are "good" by our standards, and so on. But how easy is it for us to genuinely love those who do not love us back, those who do not meet our expectations, those who hate us, those who harm us, those who insult us, those who disrespect us, those who do not value our opinion, those who do not think highly of us, or those who are not "good" in character or deeds? Not very easy, right?

Yet God's love is unconditional and unchanging. He loves even those who hate Him, those who despise Him and blaspheme His name, those who reject Him, those who do not acknowledge His existence or greatness, those who speak against Him, those who harm His followers, those who sin against Him, those who depart from Him, and those who do not meet His expectations. His great love for all mankind is displayed foremost through Jesus Christ's suffering and death on the cross. *"But God commendeth his love toward us, in that, while we were yet sinners, Christ died for us"* (Romans 5:8).

He does not stop loving us when we are disobedient or when we wander away from Him. He waits for us and draws us back toward Him in love. He understands our weaknesses and strengthens us to overcome them. He lovingly corrects us and does not allow us to be destroyed. Even our definition of love is very limited. We most often refer to love as what we feel for another person. So how a person behaves toward us greatly influences what we feel for them. God's definition of love is focused more on what is best for us. It surpasses feelings and is not merely manifested reciprocatively. That is why He gently and patiently corrects us and works in us to build us. Despite our utter wretchedness because of our sinful nature, He draws us to Himself and leads us to an eternal life with Him.

How about mercy and forgiveness? What level of wrong can we tolerate? What is the extent of our mercy and forgiveness? We may easily have mercy on someone less fortunate than us, but how smoothly does mercy flow when someone subject to our authority does something wrong (especially against us)? How about when someone dependent on us (for example, financially) turns out to be deceitful or disrespectful? How many times can we repeatedly forgive someone who has wronged us or ill-treated us? If someone keeps hurting us continually, it is not easy to keep forgiving. But God's mercy is everlasting. This is why we are not consumed by His wrath, and He gives us many opportunities to repent despite the multitude of sins that we commit daily. No matter how many times we have wronged Him or departed from Him, we can boldly approach His throne of grace and obtain mercy and forgiveness. His mercy is renewed each morning. Great is His faithfulness to us!

"It is of the LORD's mercies that we are not consumed, because his compassions fail not. They are new every morning: great is thy faithfulness" (Lamentations 3:22–23).

"For the LORD is good; his mercy is everlasting; and his truth endureth to all generations" (Psalms 100:5).

So we see that God's greatness is also displayed through all His goodness. There is no one in this world who can be as holy, good, and perfect as He is. In fact, His example gives us a good standard for these.

"O give thanks unto the Lord; for he is good:
for his mercy endureth for ever.
O give thanks unto the God of gods:
for his mercy endureth for ever.
O give thanks unto the Lord of lords:
for his mercy endureth for ever.
To him who alone doeth great wonders:
for his mercy endureth for ever.
To him that by wisdom made the heavens:
for his mercy endureth for ever.
To him that stretcheth out the earth above the waters:
for his mercy endureth for ever.
To him that made great lights:
for his mercy endureth for ever.
The sun to rule by day:
for his mercy endureth for ever.
The moon and stars to rule by night:
for his mercy endureth for ever.
Who remembered us in our low estate:
for his mercy endureth for ever:
And hath redeemed us from our enemies:
for his mercy endureth for ever.
Who giveth food to all flesh:
for his mercy endureth for ever.
O give thanks unto the God of heaven:
for his mercy endureth for ever" (Psalms 136:1–9, 23–26).

"Lift your eyes upon high and, and behold who hath created these things, that bringeth out their host by number: he calleth them all by names by the greatness of his might, for that he is strong in power; not one faileth" (Isaiah 40:26).

GOD'S WISDOM

HOW WISE IS GOD?

The LORD by wisdom hath founded the earth; by understanding hath he established the heavens.

—Proverbs 3:19

God is infinitely wise. Reflections of His wisdom are explicitly portrayed in His creative work. The most effective channel for probing into and exposing the truth about the wisdom of the Great Creator is detailed research in the four major areas of scientific study—physics, chemistry, biology, and mathematics. It is nothing but a myth that faith in God contradicts or interferes with unbiased scientific research. Research is simply a process of discovery.

Therefore, through scientific research, we only discover what God has already done in His work of creation. If our hearts are enlarged enough to search for the truth and not constricted by bias, prejudice, pride, tradition, rebellion, or stubbornness, we can marvel at many of His wondrous works when we discover what He has actually done. We can easily maintain logical thinking and sound judgment while inclining our hearts to reach a reasonable conclusion about God from what we observe in these four areas.

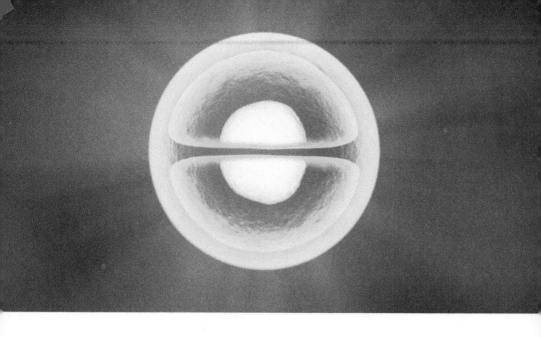

LAWS OF NATURE

As we study the four major branches of science in detail, two common themes become evident: everything in this universe is governed by *laws,* and everything has defined *measures*. Anyone who is associated with the study or application of science will agree that the universe does not operate in randomness. Things do not just happen haphazardly or in a disorderly manner or by chance. There is definite order and predictability to everything in nature.

This is achievable only because of the existence of various laws in nature and defined measures for everything. Every system and object in this universe, whether living or nonliving, follows these laws and measures and functions according to them. These maintain a certain harmony in nature such that everything runs smoothly. For example, the planets in the solar system follow the law of gravitation. They have specific orbits with defined distances from the sun. They also require defined amounts of time to orbit the sun.

Some examples of other laws that define and govern the functioning of the physical world are listed below:

Law of conservation of energy, mass, and momentum
Laws of thermodynamics
Ideal gas law
Laws of genetics
Newton's laws of motion
Fick's law of diffusion
Kirchhoff's law
Ohm's law
Coulomb's law
Law of gravitation
Laws of trigonometry
Laws of optics

There is nothing man can do to modify these laws. Through the scientific method, man discovers these laws and searches out ways to use them for our benefit. These laws and measures are the basis and reason for all of the advancements that man has made in various fields like medicine, engineering, and technology. If we were uncertain regarding how things behave or, in other words, if the *predictability* was absent, we would not have been able to build and safely operate things as we do today. Thus, we rely *fully* on these laws for things to work as intended. Without them, there is not much reason to think that we would have made any advancement in science.

But the great question is: **Who put these laws in place?**

Pythagoras Theorem

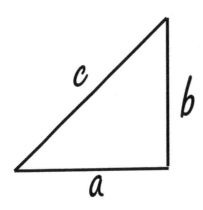

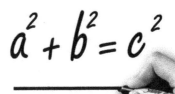

$$a^2 + b^2 = c^2$$

Man has taken thousands of years to discover these laws. There are even many laws of science and mathematics named after the people who discovered them. However, these laws and measures have always been there. These people after whom the laws were named were not the ones who made them or put them in place. For example, Newton discovered the law of gravitation; that is, there is an attractive force between two objects that is proportional to the product of their masses and inversely proportional to the square of the distance between them ($F = \frac{Gm_1m_2}{r^2}$). Although Newton was able to find this out, this law and relationship has always been there and working even before he discovered it. So through the application of the scientific method, man has only been finding out and putting to use what God has already placed in nature from the time of creation for the perfect functioning of the universe. So the point of this section is to observe the great wisdom of God in the way that He has designed things in nature.

Some Measures in Nature

Ideal Gas Law:
$$PV = nRT$$

Normal heart rate = 70 - 100 beats/min

Bernoulli's Principle:
$$P + \frac{1}{2}\rho v^2 + \rho gh = constant$$

Pressure loss in pipe:
$$\Delta p = f \frac{L}{D}\frac{\rho V^2}{2}$$

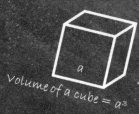

Volume of a cube = a^3

Speed of light = 3×10^8 m/s

Half life of U-235 = 7.038×10^8 years

Coulomb's Law:
Electrostatic force, $F = k\frac{q_1 q_2}{r^2}$

Newton's law:
Gravitational Force, $F = G\frac{m_1 m_2}{R^2}$

Acceleration due to gravity = 9.8 m/s^2

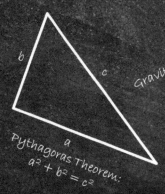

Diameter of the earth = 12, 742 km

Distance of the earth from the sun = 14.9×10^{10} m

Pythagoras Theorem:
$$a^2 + b^2 = c^2$$

Kinematic Equation:
$$d = vt + \frac{1}{2}at^2$$

Valency of sodium = 1

Number of bones in the human body = 206

Area of a Circle, $A = \pi r^2$

2nd Law of Thermodynamics:
$$\delta Q = T\,dS$$

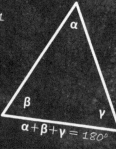

$$\alpha + \beta + \gamma = 180°$$

Number of teeth in humans = 32

Normal blood sugar = 100 mg/dL

Atomic number of silver = 47

Radius of carbon atom = 7×10^{-11} m

MEASURES IN NATURE

Where wast thou when I laid the foundations of the earth? Declare, if thou hast understanding. <u>Who hath laid the measures thereof</u>, if thou knowest?

—Job 38:4–5

When God created the universe, He defined measures for everything. These measures in the universe can be broadly categorized into two main types: constants and relationships.

Constants

These refer to unchanging numbers assigned to specific properties. For example, God has set the temperature at which water freezes to be 0°C and that at which it boils to be 100°C (at atmospheric pressure). The scale is irrelevant (Celsius, Fahrenheit, Kelvin, Rankine, etc.) since they are all just man-made ways to measure these temperatures. The point is that no matter what scale is used to measure them, these are universal unchanging measures.

Some more examples of these constants are

- physical dimensions for small and large components of nature (e.g., size of a carbon atom or size of the earth),
- measures of time (e.g., time taken for the earth for one rotation about its own axis),
- normal ranges for biological features (e.g., body temperature, chemical concentration, pulse rate, blood count, blood pressure, etc.),
- numbers for biological features (e.g., number of bones, teeth, chromosomes, etc. for each animal),
- physical properties of substances (e.g., density, molecular weight, specific heat, vapor pressure, conductivity, speed of sound, etc.),

- chemical properties of substances (e.g., valency, atomic number, half-life, etc.),
- universal constants (value of π, speed of light in vacuum, acceleration due to gravity, sum of the angles of every triangle in the world, etc.) and many other such constant measurements.

Relationships

The laws of nature are quantified by formulae that provide relationships between different parameters (e.g., Ohm's law gives the relationship between voltage, current, and resistance, the Darcy-Weisbach equation relates the pressure loss in a pipe to the average velocity of a fluid, etc.). These relationships are the basis for engineering calculations and the reason for the predictability of how things behave. By these we estimate important parameters like force, pressure, temperature, power, voltage drop, and the like and specify sizing and materials to ensure safe, reliable, and efficient operation of the systems that we design and build.

Most of these relationships are determined through experimentation. However, the most important thing to note is that these relationships between parameters like current, force, pressure, and so on that we rely heavily on for pretty much everything we build have always existed even before we discovered them, since the time that God created the world.

ENGINEERING

Engineering is simply an application of the laws and measures in nature using appropriate materials to design and construct facilities and equipment for human use and benefit. These include the homes and buildings we live and work in; the vehicles (like cars, buses, trains, ships, and planes) that we use for transportation; the roadways, railways, and bridges that we travel on; the manufacturing and power plants that we have built to process materials to make useful products or energy; the industrial equipment and machinery that we use to make work easier, better, quicker, and more efficient; the electronic items we use; the tools and appliances we use for our daily needs; and much more.

Engineering would not have been possible without (1) the predictability that is enabled by the laws and measures that govern all physical things and (2) the defined properties of each material. There is a lot of energy and many resources available to us in nature. However, we cannot benefit much from these or use them for any purpose if we cannot safely harness this energy or process and modify the available resources to beneficial forms. We can safely transform and channel the different forms of energy available to us in nature and modify the naturally occurring materials for our use and consumption because we know their physical and chemical properties and the laws that reign over them, which we use as reins to manipulate, control, and transform them to useful forms.

For example, one of the most common forms of energy that we use every day is electricity. This electricity is typically generated from other naturally occurring forms of energy like wind energy, or the kinetic energy of flowing water, or the energy derived from the combustion of fossil fuels, and so forth. This conversion can be done only because of the *law of electromagnetic induction*. This law states that an electromotive force will be generated in an electrical conductor in a changing magnetic field. If this law did not exist, we would not be able to generate electricity for our large-scale use as we do it today. This law was discovered by Faraday. But needless to say, he was not

responsible for it being there. It had always been there. In the same way, the photovoltaic effect of solar energy on certain materials also allows us to generate electricity.

It is well known that electricity is a very dangerous form of energy that can cause serious injury and/or death. However, after generating it in a power plant, we are still able to distribute it in a safe and controlled manner to different users for consumption only because we know precisely how it behaves; that is, we know the laws that govern it. For example, we know that we need thicker wires to handle larger current flow. So we have developed minimum standards to follow in sizing conductors. We also use this principle for designing fuses as a means of protection (overcurrent leads to melting of metal and interruption of current flow). We also know that certain materials are good conductors and good insulators of electricity. So we cover them with a protective layer of insulating material if there is a potential (no pun intended) for them to be touched.

Thus, we can use these laws and properties and other things we have learnt about electricity to safely harness electrical energy to our advantage. We can bring this energy to our homes, buildings, and other facilities to power our machines and equipment, keep our lights shining, run our appliances, and charge our computers. If these laws and relations were not in place and if electricity did not behave *the same way all the time* and if material properties were constantly changing, this would not have been possible.

In the same manner, we can use the energy generated by the controlled combustion of petrol or other hydrocarbons in closed chambers to power our fast-moving vehicles. We can do this because of the properties of the fuel that generates enough energy on combustion and the certainty we have in the physical integrity of the engine that guarantees the safety of the whole process. Although operating equipment powered by continuous mini-explosions in front of us (i.e., driving a car) has become so much a part of our daily life, it is still a thing of marvel.

In the same way, if Bernoulli's principle did not exist, we would not be able to fly airplanes as we do today. If Newton's third law of motion did not exist, we would not be able to launch a rocket into space as we do today. If the Joule-Thompson effect did not exist, refrigeration and air-conditioning would not have been possible. If the laws associated with statics did not exist, we could not build bridges as we do today. If we did not have confidence in the strength of materials or their other physical and chemical properties, we could not have been using them for building our buildings, boats, bridges, planes, process plants, rockets, and so forth.

So all the wonders of engineering and technology that we enjoy today are only due to the fact that we have learnt through experimentation, research, and trial-and-error methods to make use of the properties of materials and the laws that God has embedded in the functioning of natural things. Hopefully, I have encouraged a few young minds to pursue this fascinating world of engineering that glorifies God so much in a not-so-obvious way.

MATERIALS

The physical world is made up of several different types of materials. Each material has its own physical and chemical properties which are determined by its structure and chemical composition. There are about 118 different elements in nature known to man today.[12] Naturally existing materials may consist of molecules of the same element or compounds formed by the combination of different elements. The atomic and molecular structure (number of electrons, valency, types of bonding, types of crystalline structure, etc.) will determine the properties exhibited by each material. It is undoubtedly a wondrous thing that there is so much order in the world even down to the atomic and nuclear level. So much so that the physical and chemical properties of every material is predictable based on its molecular structure and chemical composition.

Over the years, man has been successful in identifying the different elements and their physical and chemical properties mainly through repeated experimentation. For example, we know what will happen when we mix different chemicals. We have studied the kinetics of many reactions. We have been able to determine physical properties (for example, melting and boiling points) of different substances. We have developed thermodynamic data and charts for various substances. We know the electrical resistivity and conductivity for different materials. We have developed stress-strain curves and determined tensile strength for metals, and so on. Through this process, we have been able to discover the favorable properties of many materials that can be used to our advantage. In other words, our understanding of material properties helps us decide what should be used for what purpose.

We are able to use these materials only because we know their properties—what they are good for and unsuitable for. We know that these properties will never change; that is, their behavior in a given set of conditions is always predictable. Again, this predictability is valuable in helping us assign materials to definite applications. For example, we know copper is a very good conductor of electricity, so we use it for electrical wiring. We know

Some common materials that we use—concrete, steel, graphite, copper, gold, brass, plastics, wood, cotton, ceramics, paper, galvanized iron, cardboard, granite, glass, wool, polystyrene, and aluminum.

that methane (natural gas) has properties that are desirable (e.g., clean burning, suitable heating value, etc.) for its use as a domestic fuel for cooking and heating in our homes.

Thus, man has had great success over the centuries in discovering what's good for what and conducting extensive research and testing to optimize the use of materials in engineering applications. However, we cannot take any credit for assigning any of these properties to materials. We must offer credit for their properties and their dependability to the One Who ordained structures and properties to all materials.

Synthetic Materials

We have also been successful in "making" new materials (like alloys, polymers, etc.) by converting naturally available materials to synthetic ones that have superior properties for our applications. For example, we have been able to make long chain polymers (e.g., plastics like PVC, Teflon, polyethylene, Kevlar, etc.) from smaller hydrocarbon molecules, which have many applications like electrical insulation, piping, packaging, and the like. We have been able to make steel by the addition of elements like carbon, nickel, chromium, and manganese to iron in varying amounts to enhance the properties of this material based on the application. Other examples include the manufacture of vulcanized rubber by the addition of sulfur; semiconductors by doping silicon with boron and phosphorus; cement by mixing lime, silica, alumina, and so forth; and many other synthetic materials. Thus, we have successfully identified the effect of modifications such as mixing, reacting, heating, pressurizing, treating, and other processes to many naturally occurring materials to obtain better materials with superior properties for use in specific engineering applications. However, we should be able to easily admit that *God is responsible for the properties of the base materials and also for the superior properties of the resultant synthetic materials.* We have discovered *what to do* to make things better. But we are not the ones responsible for the resultant qualities of any synthetic material we have "created."

So we can sincerely thank God for every small and large thing that we use and enjoy today—our watches, cell phones, colognes, computers, houses, cars, roads, air conditioners, chairs, tables, appliances, musical instruments…the list is unending.

MEDICINE

The field of medicine has advanced greatly over the past few centuries and is still progressing. Methods to diagnose, heal, repair, and restore the ill and injured have been studied extensively. For this, many natural and synthetic materials have been identified to support, supplement, or supplant the chemicals and organisms in the body and bring it back to a normal state. Procedures and methods for testing and treatment have been developed and are being used by experts trained on the anatomical and physiological details of the human body.

It may go unnoticed that the field of medicine is a combination of the application of the laws of physics, chemistry, and biology. Take the field of diagnostic testing for example. We are able to understand much about the effect of microorganisms on the body and diagnose diseases that are caused by them through medical examinations. If we did not have the laws of optics, we would not even have been able to use a simple microscope. We are able to perform other diagnostic tests like ultrasounds, x-ray, CT scans, MRI, and the like only because of the laws of physics that enabled the development of each technology. We may perhaps take pride in discovering these methods and developing the technology for them, but these are only possible due to the laws that God placed in nature. We should be thankful to God for these laws that have enabled us to see and know the things about our bodies beyond our natural limitations.

The human body is also subject to many biological laws. There is a specific way and pattern that the body must behave and function. Different parameters within the body are defined by definite measures. We compare everything to these measures to determine if there is disease. Reliable diagnosis is only possible because the standard functions and measures of the human body are known and unchanging. For example, if the body temperature exceeds the normal value of 37°C, we know there is a fever. If the blood sugar level exceeds the normal range of 100–110 mg/dL, we suspect diabetes. We chart

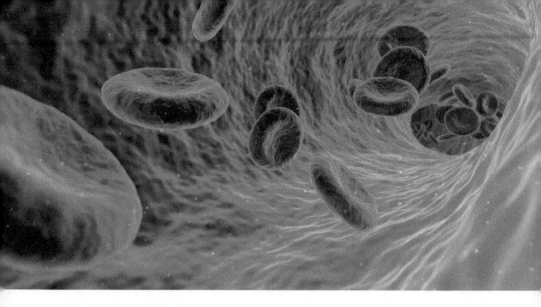

the heart's performance and compare it to a known standard to see if there is any sign of disease. In the same manner, we know the normal or expected behavior of each organ. We suspect disease and treat it when there is a deviation from the known standard functions and measures. In addition to all these medical methods of diagnosis, God has also designed mechanisms in our body to alert us of disease (symptoms like fever and pain).

Much of the modern treatment methods that we employ today are possible only because the body is governed by laws. For example, if the body did not have a self-healing nature or if blood did not have a property of clotting, we would not be able to conduct surgeries very well. This self-healing nature and other functional aspects of the body are so amazing. Perhaps we just don't think much of it because of how we are used to seeing it so often. When we get a cut on our skin, what a blessing it is that the body automatically stops the blood flow through clotting and grows new skin to heal the open wound. This is a truly awesome feature of the human body. How many of man's inventions have this self-repairing capability? Yet we say that all this evolved through random, unassisted changes?

Over the years, we have studied and discovered the chemical composition and physical functioning of the human body, which runs better than any man-made machine, automated plant, or factory. We have also understood the effect of different chemicals on the body (dose and response) and have even been able to develop physiologically based pharmacokinetic (PBPK) models to simulate these effects on each organ. We have applied this knowledge, along with years of experimentation and experience, to use these chemicals (known as drugs or medicines) to treat disease. As a result, we created the pharmaceutical industry. These dose-response relationships between drugs and the body (i.e., specific effects of specific chemicals on the body) are a characteristic feature of the body itself. Although we have discovered these relationships through hundreds, maybe thousands of years of research, the laws of pharmacology were ordained by the all-knowing Creator of the human body. So if we must marvel, let us marvel at His wisdom.

AGRICULTURE

We cannot live without food. This body of ours needs energy and nutrition to run all its complex functions and to just survive. To meet this need that is common to every human and animal that inhabits planet earth and to sustain life on earth, God created natural systems that enable the manufacture of food in plants.

The word *manufacture* is being deliberately used here. This is to emphasize that this process is comparable to the process taking place in a man-made manufacturing plant where raw materials are converted to useful products using different processes and forms of energy! In nature, this is done through the process of photosynthesis. The plant or tree draws the raw materials (nutrients and water) from the soil and uses the energy from the sun to manufacture different varieties of food, depending on what tree or plant it is. Humans do assist, enhance, and accelerate this process externally in various levels like releasing pollinators, adding soil fertilizers, irrigation, soil conditioning, allowing access to the sun's energy, and so forth. But the internal process of producing edible food is completely unaided and

uninfluenced by humans. This is a miracle we have been witnessing and perhaps taking for granted for thousands and thousands of years!

As we discussed much earlier in this book, God also gave diverse varieties of fruits and vegetables with diverse tastes, shapes, textures, colors, smells, and the like so that not just our bodies' need for nutrition is met, but our hearts are also satisfied. We can choose what we would like to eat and cook them in different ways to enhance their taste to suit our taste buds during each meal. Another great design feature related to food is the way that God has given us natural indicators like smell or color to easily detect when food has spoiled and is no longer fit for our consumption!

"And God said, let the earth bring forth grass, the herb yielding seed, and the fruit tree yielding fruit after his kind, whose seed is in itself, upon the earth: and it was so. And the earth brought forth grass, and herb yielding seed after his kind, and the tree yielding fruit, whose seed was in itself, after his kind: and God saw that it was good" (Genesis 1:11–12).

Food production is not the only miracle associated with a plant's life cycle. I am also fascinated by how a seed sown in the

ground germinates to form a seedling. We treat this as an automatic function in nature, but it is an amazing functionality that God has incorporated into the natural world to facilitate the reproduction of plants. Through this process, the supply of food for man and animals is maintained continuously.

"And that which thou sowest, thou knowest not that body that shall be, but bare grain, it may be chance of wheat, or of some other grain: But God giveth it a body as it hath pleased him, and to every seed his own body" (1 Corinthians 15:37–38).

The process of pollination is also amazing. Plants and trees, as we know, are stationary. Since they cannot move, they need a way to transfer pollen from the anther of a male flower to the stigma of a female flower (for cross-pollination). God has designed a brilliant solution for this in nature. Wind and pollinators like bees and butterflies help transfer the pollen to distant flowers and thereby enable fertilization. This fertilization process is essential for producing seeds and fruit. This is an incredible solution to a problem that could potentially have left us hungry and without enough food for sustenance.

Without any experience in farming or technology, all species of herbivorous, carnivorous, and omnivorous animals have been finding food for their sustenance for thousands and thousands of years since their creation. Is it not amazing that God's design of this world included natural processes to maintain a steady food supply for His creation? Well, if you think about it, why would He do it any other way? No, it should not be surprising that His creative work provided all things that are needed to sustain His creation.

We have now learned to mass-produce various types of food to sustain ourselves (and in fact, have surplus in most parts of the world) through the use of agricultural machinery and our knowledge of the laws that govern agriculture. We are able to make genetic modifications and make even hybrid varieties for better yield and quality. The DNA and genetic makeup of plants and the properties assigned to each gene were determined by God. God has done this also by His wisdom.

LIFE

And the LORD *God formed man of the dust of the ground, and breathed into his nostrils the breath of life; and man became a living soul.*

—Genesis 2:7

Human life and its many inexplicable mysteries are interesting to ponder upon. We define life as the period we spend on earth being able to breathe and function physically and mentally. When our heart stops beating and when we stop breathing, our life ends. Yet our life is much more than just the physical functioning of the body and its organs (heart, brain, lungs, etc.). The human body is known to be physically made up of organic and inorganic chemicals. There are many chemical reactions and processes that enable the body to function and be alive. But man is not just a body that runs like a machine. If so, death may have been preventable and reversible. If a machine stops functioning, it can be repaired and restored by fixing the defect that caused it. Machines do not usually "die" just because one component stops working. No human has found (or ever will find) a way to prevent or return from death. So death is much more than a physical cessation of the functioning of the body's organs. We are alive because God has given us a spirit within us. We die when that spirit departs from the body. God is the One Who gives us this spirit (and life) and takes it away from our bodies. This is *irreversible* and *unpreventable* for all humans.

Some evidence for human life being more than physical things is seen through the abstract, intangible, and invisible things that we experience in life. We all have a mind and a spirit within us. We also refer to the heart as the place that houses our feelings and emotions. So the things that spring from these—thoughts, motives, desires, emotions, love, memories, imaginations, dreams of the night, and the conscience (judging between good and bad, right and wrong)— are not mere chemical processes. Although we know that some of these are processed in the brain, they are intangible, invisible, and mostly inexplicable in physical terms. Have you ever realized that one person's thoughts, memories, or dreams can never ever be visualized by another person? Yet God sees all these for every single individual who ever lived.

THE HUMAN BODY

For thou hast possessed my reins: thou hast covered me in my mother's womb. I will praise thee; for I am fearfully and wonderfully made: marvellous are thy works; and that my soul knoweth right well.

—Psalms 139:13–14

This temporary physical dwelling place for man's spirit; that is, the human body, is by itself marvelous. This is true of all of God's creation. The bodies that God has given to man, animals, and different organisms are wondrously fashioned. The general and specific design features of every organ, tissue, cell, and the like are engineered to perfection. The closer we examine and discover these anatomical and physiological features, the more cause for praise we accumulate. These design features are intentional and not coincidental since they serve specific purposes. To simplify our discussion, however, let's focus just on the human body as it is most relevant for us and probably the easiest for us to understand and relate to.

The human body is more complex than any computer, electronic device, machinery, processing plant, or factory that man has ever made.

To accentuate this complexity, let us try and compare the human body to a man-made plant (e.g., refinery, gas processing plant, petrochemicals plant, manufacturing plant, etc.). All the systems and organs in the human body and their functions surpass the engineering design involved in the construction of even the largest operating man-made plant in the world. To add to this, the human body is self-sustaining and comparatively low-maintenance considering its size, complexity, and "design life."

Design

The design of a complex man-made plant takes years to complete. It goes through many reviews and revisions until the final design is approved for construction. This is the time to implement ideas and identify errors. Things are easier to fix on paper than when they are being built! There are many people involved in the design process. The success of the project depends heavily on who is involved in the design phase and how well the plant has been designed. A well-designed plant will need expert contributions from highly competent and well-experienced engineers, operators, maintenance personnel, and managers.

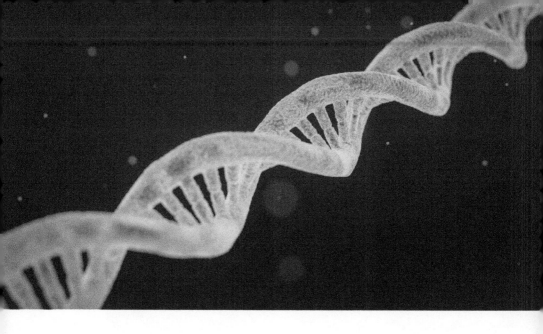

The design of the fully automated plant that is the human body is predetermined and completed by the Great Designer, God. There is obviously no question about His competency (wisdom) as is evidently displayed in His creation and highlighted again and again in this section of this book. The body's design is embedded in its genetic makeup, that is, the DNA blueprint. This DNA blueprint has specific, meaningful, coded information that determines the unique features of that body. Whenever we see nonrandom, meaningful information (e.g., a poem, a book, a letter, engineering drawings, computer code, etc.), would it be logical or illogical for us to assume that there is an author or engineer(s) responsible for the information? Why, then, is it considered such a far-fetched and illogical notion that God has designed our amazing bodies? Not only designed it but also engraved the design information (DNA) in our bodies for us to see, use, and marvel!

Construction (The Miracle of Birth)

The construction phase of a project sees the implementation of the design of the plant. This phase takes a lot of hard work and coordination. The right equipment must be purchased and laid out as per design. A lot of skilled labor is employed so that construction quality can be maintained per requirements, and errors can be min-

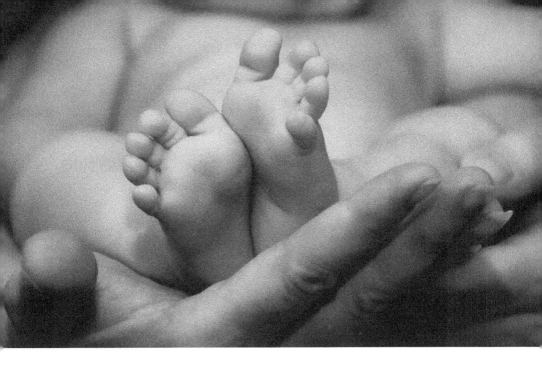

imized. The construction phase also requires several reviews, inspections, and testing to ensure all components are installed as per design and specification. Commissioning is required to ensure everything runs properly and there are no safety concerns. The construction, commissioning, and start-up of a plant can take years to complete.

Compared to a man-made plant, the human body is constructed fairly quickly. The whole process takes only about nine months to complete, and there are billions of such "plants" in the world! They all function the same way, and their components are very much similar. The whole construction process for the human body takes place mostly unaided in the mother's womb. Other than supplying nutrition, ensuring safety, monitoring progress, and preparing for birth, there is not much that we can do to facilitate (or accelerate) growth inside the womb. There is no coordination or skill required from our part that can influence its progress. The majority of "labor" that is required is at the time of childbirth (not saying that pregnancy is an easy process)! Growth happens *on its own* right from the time of conception. In fact, even conception is such a blessing and gift from God.

"Lo, children are an heritage of the LORD: and the fruit of the womb is his reward" (Psalms 127:3).

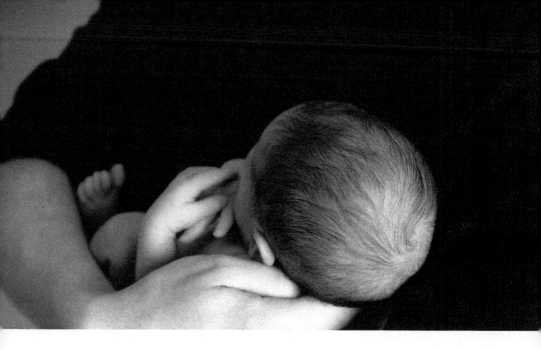

The construction process for the human body starts when an egg becomes fertilized and forms a zygote that becomes an embryo, then a fetus, and finally a baby who is born into the world. The single cell that is formed at conception divides into two and then multiplies by further divisions. From one single cell, millions and millions of cells form. As the divisions progress, they eventually get "automatically" grouped as tissues and further develop to form the different organs and components of the body like skin, brain, heart, eyes, bones, blood, and so forth. Each has its own size, proportion, count (measure), texture, appearance, and function. No one can explain what drives a single-celled zygote to divide so perfectly and form cells, tissues, and organs. Without any external human influence other than proper nutrition and adequate care to prevent any external damaging influence, the embryo by itself has the capability to transform from a tiny, barely detectable dot to a fully developed human baby within the gestation period allotted to humans—about forty weeks.

"As thou knowest not what is the way of the spirit, nor how the bones do grow in the womb of her that is with child: even so thou knowest not the works of God who maketh all" (Ecclesiastes 11:5).

No one can supervise or direct this standard process that happens in every human womb that conceives. We can only run occasional scans and observe progress, but God directs this process for every single individual who is conceived, and He determines what should come out. Not only that, but He also gives a spirit to each individual person at conception. This cannot be explained in biological terms.

Systems, Subsystems, and Components

It is common to divide a plant into different systems or units for better documentation and maintenance. For example, a natural gas plant may consist of systems like separation, dehydration, sulfur-removal, instrument air, nitrogen, electrical, fresh water, wastewater, and the like. These can be further divided into subsystems like compressor units, separators, filters, absorbers, and so forth. Each subsystem would have different components like vessels, pumps, piping, instruments, local control panels, and the like.

To continue our comparison with a man-made plant, the human body can also be divided into different systems like the skeletal, nervous, respiratory, circulatory systems, and so forth. These systems also have subsystems, which include organs, nerves, blood vessels, and the like. Each subsystem has smaller components like tissues, cells, enzymes, hormones, and so forth. Let us look at some of these systems and components.

Structural System

Every plant will need to have a structural system consisting of foundations, steel and concrete supports, beams, clamps, and so forth to set equipment and piping. This ensures that the components are installed levelly, will remain fixed in place, and resist movement due to vibration, fluid flow, and other loads applied on them. Although slightly different in comparison to a man-made plant, the body also has a structural system. The skeletal system provides support to the organs of the body. The bones, tendons, ligaments, and the like protect the organs that are housed in the body, provide structure and rigidity, enable movement, and provide the ability to perform tasks.

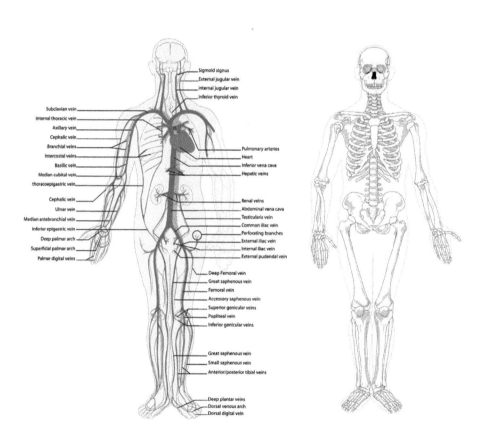

Sigmoid signus
External jugular vein
Internal jugular vein
Inferior thyroid vein

Subclavian vein
Internal thoracic vein
Axillary vein
Cephalic vein
Branchial veins
Intercostal veins
Basilic vein
Median cubital vein
thoracoepigastric vein

Pulmonary arteries
Heart
Inferior vena cava
Hepatic veins

Cephalic vein
Ulnar vein
Median antebranchial vein
Inferior epigastric vein
Deep palmar arch
Superficial palmar arch
Palmar digital veins

Renal veins
Abdominal vena cava
Testicularis vein
Common iliac vein
Perforating branches
External iliac vein
Internal iliac vein
External pudendal vein

Deep Femoral vein
Great saphenous vein
Femoral vein
Accessory saphenous vein
Superior genicular veins
Popliteal vein
Inferior genicular veins

Great saphenous vein
Small saphenous vein
Anterior/posterior tibial veins

Deep plantar veins
Dorsal venous arch
Dorsal digital vein

Material Transport

In a plant, materials like oil, gas, chemicals, air, and water are transported through a system of piping. Pumps and compressors are required to increase pressure and ensure that flow is maintained as required. There is an amazingly similar "piping system" in our bodies. Materials in the body (blood, oxygen, digested food, chemicals, hormones, waste, etc.) are transported to organs and cells for use through the circulatory system, which consists of a simple, powerful, and reliable central positive displacement pump (heart) and a system of piping (blood vessels). Material transfer at the points of reception is achieved mainly through membranes by diffusion.

Process Control

An automated plant operates through a process control system, which may consist of a centralized Distributed Control System (DCS), Process Logic Controllers (PLCs), sensors, instrumentation, control valves, associated cables, and so forth. The instruments sense and transmit information to the DCS or PLCs via wires and cables.

The DCS or PLCs process this information and send commands to the control valves via wires and cables so that desired set points are maintained for various parameters like flow rate, level, pressure, temperature, and the like.

In the body, process control is done primarily by the nervous system. In this system, the brain performs functions similar to a DCS or PLC as the centralized process controller. The sensors in our body (sense organs like eyes, ears, nose, skin, etc.) behave like the sensors and instrumentation in a plant and pick up information (optical, vibratory or sound, chemical, etc.). The nerves in our body function like the wires and cables that transmit information in a plant. The brain receives information from the sensory organs and other sources that are transmitted as electrical signals through a distributed system of nerves. The brain processes this information and sends commands as electrical signals to "control devices" like organs, muscles, glands, and so forth to perform functions and/or to maintain normal operating set points in the body.

A simple example of a feedback process control loop in our body would be how the pituitary and thyroid glands maintain T3 and T4 hormone levels in the blood. These hormones are required by our cells for metabolism. When their levels in the blood drop, the pituitary gland senses this and produces the thyroid stimulating hormone (TSH). This hormone stimulates the thyroid gland to produce more T3 and T4 hormones. When sufficient levels are reached, the pituitary gland decreases TSH production and thus regulates the

T3 and T4 levels in the blood. Doctors use TSH levels in the blood as an indicator to gauge and understand thyroid gland health and functioning. Process control systems in man-made plants are fairly recent advancements. As with other things, the technology has been improving as the years progress. Yet God has included perfectly functioning process control systems in our bodies from the time of creation thousands of years ago.

Waste Management

Every product or by-product in a processing plant may not be desired or useful. In fact, there may be some materials that are removed as part of the process because they contaminate or harm the desired products, or they are unwanted by-products. This generates waste streams that must be appropriately handled. Thus, in order to properly run a plant, waste management is essential. Without this, the plant would not be able to run for too long. So almost every plant has a waste disposal or treatment system of some sort (e.g., thermal oxidizers, flares, water treatment facilities, injection wells, tanks for temporary storage, solid waste disposal, etc.).

The human body is also designed with a waste management and disposal system. This consists of the digestive and urinary systems, which include components like the intestines, kidneys, and liver that function to process and dispose the toxic and undesired materials as waste from the body. This is very critical to the proper functioning of the body just like in any plant.

Energy

In order to run all the equipment in a plant, some form of energy is essential. Normally, most of the equipment is powered by electricity. The plant may have its own power generation system (using diesel, steam, gas, and so forth as energy sources) or may draw it from the local power grid.

God made a way for the human body to generate its own energy to perform all its functions. This is done through complex processes that take place in the cells that help convert the food that we eat to energy.

Plant Upsets

If a plant deviates drastically or significantly from its normal operating conditions, it is termed as an "upset" condition. Some of the systems may need repair or maintenance. Sometimes, immediate action may be required to prevent further damage or incidents. Sometimes, the entire plant would have to be shut down and necessary inspections completed. When the body is in an upset condition (called disease), sometimes a shutdown (rest) and additional maintenance (surgery, treatment, therapy, etc.) needs to be done for recovery back to normal operations. The body has its own "maintenance personnel" (immune system) like leukocytes (WBC) that search out and destroy disease-causing agents and its own self-repair and recovery functionality.

There are many amazingly designed systems, organs, and functions of the human body that we have not discussed here. The point I am trying to make is that the human body is so well designed with

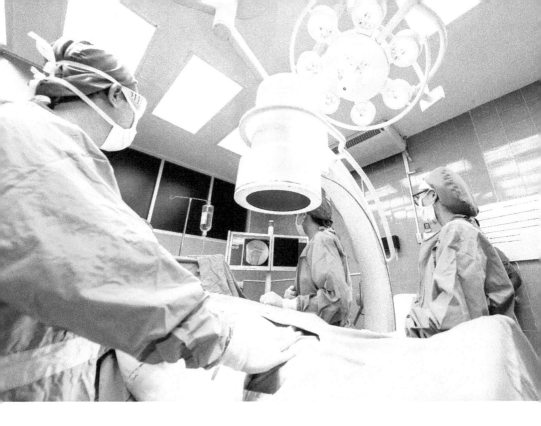

very complex components and functions. Studying the anatomy and physiology of the human body should cause us to ponder much about God's brilliance and engineering excellence! When we look at a man-made plant, we would never be inclined to suggest that all this was an accident or the result of random, unassisted coincidences. Yet we accept this explanation for things much, much more complex in the natural world.

LIFE PROCESSES AND SYSTEMS

We can see various examples of God's wisdom in the way that He placed us on this earth with biological and physical systems and conditions suitable for the sustenance of life. This is observed from the macroscale to the microscale. For example, as discussed earlier, the earth is at optimum distance from the sun, which allows us to be at the right temperature and use the sun's energy to our advantage. Through the revolution of the earth around its own axis and around the sun, He made a way for us to measure time (days and years). We depend a lot on this measure for our day-to-day activities. He divided the day from the night so that we can work and do our activities and then rest. This regular rest at night is required for our bodies to remain healthy and function effectively.

He made ecosystems and provided suitable habitats for each animal to live in. He made plants and trees to manufacture food on a large scale through the process of photosynthesis so that we can be nourished, be healthy, and grow. We can digest the food we eat and convert it to energy in the body through many biological systems, enzymes, cycles, reactions, and so forth. He made seasons for us to sow and to reap. He maintains a continuous supply of rain for us and keeps the rivers flowing through the water cycle, which operates like an automatic fountain through the processes of evaporation and condensation. There are many more examples to speak of regarding the systems and processes God has placed in nature like the earth's rotation (daytime and nighttime), wind circuits, ocean currents, seasons, reproduction in plants, microorganisms, animals and man, and many more. All these systems run in perfect harmony (like clockwork, except for the disruptions we ourselves have introduced).

In the book of Job (in the Bible), God asks Job many questions while describing His wisdom in creating the creatures and systems of the natural world. He describes His power displayed in them and His care for them.

This chapter is quoted below:

"Then the Lord answered Job out of the whirlwind, and said,

Who is this that darkeneth counsel by words without knowledge?

Gird up now thy loins like a man; for I will demand of thee, and answer thou me.

Where wast thou when I laid the foundations of the earth? declare, if thou hast understanding.

Who hath laid the measures thereof, if thou knowest? or who hath stretched the line upon it?

Whereupon are the foundations thereof fastened? or who laid the corner stone thereof;

When the morning stars sang together, and all the sons of God shouted for joy?

Or who shut up the sea with doors, when it brake forth, as if it had issued out of the womb?

When I made the cloud the garment thereof, and thick darkness a swaddlingband for it,

And brake up for it my decreed place, and set bars and doors,

And said, Hitherto shalt thou come, but no further: and here shall thy proud waves be stayed?

Hast thou commanded the morning since thy days; and caused the dayspring to know his place;

That it might take hold of the ends of the earth, that the wicked might be shaken out of it?

It is turned as clay to the seal; and they stand as a garment.

And from the wicked their light is withholden, and the high arm shall be broken.

Hast thou entered into the springs of the sea? or hast thou walked in the search of the depth?

Have the gates of death been opened unto thee? or hast thou seen the doors of the shadow of death?

Hast thou perceived the breadth of the earth? declare if thou knowest it all.

Where is the way where light dwelleth? and as for darkness, where is the place thereof,

That thou shouldest take it to the bound thereof, and that thou shouldest know the paths to the house thereof?

Knowest thou it, because thou wast then born? or because the number of thy days is great?

Hast thou entered into the treasures of the snow? or hast thou seen the treasures of the hail,

Which I have reserved against the time of trouble, against the day of battle and war?

By what way is the light parted, which scattereth the east wind upon the earth?

Who hath divided a watercourse for the overflowing of waters, or a way for the lightning of thunder;

To cause it to rain on the earth, where no man is; on the wilderness, wherein there is no man;

Out of whose womb came the ice? and the hoary frost of heaven, who hath gendered it?

The waters are hid as with a stone, and the face of the deep is frozen.

Canst thou bind the sweet influences of Pleiades, or loose the bands of Orion?

To satisfy the desolate and waste ground; and to cause the bud of the tender herb to spring forth?

Hath the rain a father? or who hath begotten the drops of dew?

Canst thou bring forth Mazzaroth in his season? or canst thou guide Arcturus with his sons?

Knowest thou the ordinances of heaven? canst thou set the dominion thereof in the earth?

Canst thou lift up thy voice to the clouds, that abundance of waters may cover thee?

Canst thou send lightnings, that they may go and say unto thee, Here we are?

Who hath put wisdom in the inward parts? or who hath given understanding to the heart?

Who can number the clouds in wisdom? or who can stay the bottles of heaven,

When the dust groweth into hardness, and the clods cleave fast together?

Wilt thou hunt the prey for the lion? or fill the appetite of the young lions,

When they couch in their dens, and abide in the covert to lie in wait?

Who provideth for the raven his food? when his young ones cry unto God, they wander for lack of meat" (Job 38:1–41).

THOSE AMAZING ANIMALS
(AND PLANTS)

All of nature is full of awe-inspiring creatures. It is estimated that there are about 8.7 million species on the earth.[13] Now this number includes all known life-forms like plants, birds, animals, insects, microorganisms, and others; but that is still quite a large number. My high school biology lessons would have been much more interesting if I had realized just how much these species display God's wisdom through His perfection in their design.

Careful study of the features, functions, and behaviors of these creatures really unravels His ingenuity. They are fitted and programmed with many design features that allow them to perform their required functions and interact with other animals and their surroundings in their ecosystems. Many features often get brushed off as adaptation, which may be true to a relatively small extent. But the truth is that these are inbuilt capabilities and design features that were purposely programmed into the behaviors and bodily functions of these creatures by their wise Creator. The examples that follow are just a few things that I have picked as being interesting features and behaviors of plants and animals. There are certainly many more that deserve a place on the list below.

Cuttlefish. I have watched videos (in amazement) that show the brilliant color-changing tactics of the cuttlefish that camouflages itself for protection against predators. These creatures are able to mimic the colors and patterns of their surrounding environment. They are so well hidden sometimes that they are quite unrecognizable. They also have an inbuilt defense mechanism by which they squirt an inklike substance to confuse their attacker. Similarly, there are many other creatures that are good at camouflaging themselves by blending into their surroundings (for example, some frogs, stick insects, owls, etc.). The chameleon is probably the most famous among the color-changing animals.

Mantis shrimp. The mantis shrimp is being studied closely by researchers because of an amazing and unique feature in its design. It can deliver an extremely powerful blow (sufficient to break the glass

Termites build engineered skyscrapers that can be as tall as thirty feet!

of an aquarium) by storing potential energy in its claw with a springlike mechanism. When it releases the spring, the claw moves so fast that it creates a shock wave.

Tendrils. Back in your vegetable or fruit garden, have you observed how a vine creeps along and extends its tendrils like fingers to affix itself to another tree's branch? I have found it very interesting to watch these creepers slowly climb on to other trees or man-made supports using their fingerlike tendrils. What a fascinating feature God has given for these plants to spread themselves!

Nature's architects. Have you noticed the skill with which a weaver bird builds its nest? Have you thought about how a beaver builds a *watertight* dam in the middle of the water? These beavers are intelligent engineers that know exactly what to do to build and maintain their homes in the middle of the water. Termites build amazingly engineered structures for their colonies, which can be considered as skyscrapers for their size (even as tall as thirty feet). These buildings are designed with a ventilation system that has been mimicked by humans for designing self-cooled buildings. The intricate network of tunnels and chimneys allow their dwelling to be maintained within a specific temperature range despite very high temperatures outside. These structures are so elaborately designed within with architectural ingenuity that far surpasses the expectation we have for such tiny and simple creatures. Recently, I watched a video[14] where an underground megalopolis of ants was uncovered by some scientists. This megacity, going as deep as eight meters (about twenty-six feet) beneath the earth, was constructed by one of the tiniest creatures on earth. The scientists poured about ten tons of cement for three days to discover the intricate structure of their city, which consisted of subterranean highways, side roads, and large chambers all constructed by ants!

Bees. Have you thought about how busy bees manufacture sweet honey from nectar? When a bee discovers nectar, it goes back to the hive and informs the other bees of its discovery. It communicates the exact location and quality of the honey to the other bees through a series of dances and movements! It's amazing to watch how God designed this communication method in these small crea-

tures. After collecting nectar from the flowers, the worker bees store it in their stomachs and pass it on to other bees. These bees transfer the collected nectar to geometrically perfect hexagonal honeycomb structures that they construct out of wax made in their bodies. This construction process itself is quite interesting. Here, the bees flap their wings over the honey to dehydrate it. The honey is then sealed with beeswax and stored in the honeycomb.

Spider or silkworm silk. Spiders are often viewed as creepy insects. It is quite unpleasant to walk into a spider's web. But the silk used to make this web is yet another amazing part of God's creation. The spider manufactures many different types of silk within its body for different applications! A sticky kind is weaved into a netlike pattern to trap its prey. Another kind is used to make a protective sac around its eggs and another as a dragline. The spider makes its silk through tiny organs called spinnerets and releases them when needed. Spider silk is one of the strongest materials in nature. I was fascinated to discover that some people have devoted their whole careers to studying how spiders make silk! More on this is covered in the biomimicry section. The silkworms, in the same manner, manufacture quite a popular textile material for us—silk! This silk is made in their bodies by silk glands and ejected through spinnerets to construct their cocoons.

Water spider. The diving bell spider (or water spider) lives almost entirely underwater. It does so by carrying an air bubble around its abdomen just like we would carry a scuba tank for diving. This little creature was doing this even before humans started using scuba tanks for diving! This spider also builds a nest underwater that behaves like an air chamber. It does this using its silk and by collecting air from above the surface of the water and depositing it in the chamber.

Archer fish. The archer fish lurks close to the surface of the water and shoots its prey down with remarkable accuracy (usually insects above the surface of the water) with a jet of water from its mouth. It does this by pressing its tongue against a groove in the roof of its mouth. While taking aim and calculating the position of its target, it needs to correct for the refraction of light through the water. So it is quite amazing that it rarely misses!

Motion. Bacteria propagate through viscous media using flagella, which are powered by flagellar motors that spin at the base. These motors are extremely powerful and can quickly change direction. The wings and bones of a bird are specially designed for flight. The streamlined structure and shapes of fishes are designed to enable smooth movement in water. Humans are studying these features to better design our cars and planes for more efficient operation. Did you know that the cheetah, the fastest animal, can accelerate from 0–60 miles per hour in just three seconds? It is designed with special features for running such as its springlike, flexible spine, long legs, small head, and long tail for balance.

Compound eyes. Many insects see through compound eyes (e.g., housefly). These are comprised of thousands of photoreceptor units, which produce images that are combined to enable vision for these insects. Humans and most animals have simple eyes, which itself is not so simple considering the optical technology it uses in producing an image on the retina and conveying that to the brain through the optic nerve.

Giraffes. Some animals have special mechanisms to address some unique situations. A giraffe's heart pumps at higher pressures in order to be able to overcome the hydrostatic pressure of the blood in its neck and send the blood to its brain. However, when it bends down to drink some water, there is a risk of rupturing its blood vessels because there is no hydrostatic pressure to overcome. God designed a system of valves in the giraffe's circulatory system (in its neck) to prevent this overpressure and rupture potential.

Defense. There are some inbuilt defense mechanisms in some creatures that are quite interesting. For example, the skunk releases strong-smelling chemicals to ward off predators while sea creatures like the octopus stores ink in its body and releases it to make a quick escape. The bombardier beetle makes a bomb within its body by mixing hydroquinone and hydrogen peroxide (along with other chemicals) and ejects it effectively for self-defense.

Instincts at birth. There are many things that animals or humans do not have to be taught at birth. These are instincts that they are born with. For example, the basic need for survival is met when a newly born baby animal finds a way to drink milk from its mother. It is not possible to teach a human baby how to drink when it is born, but right from birth, the baby knows how to suck and drink from its mother (or a bottle). The baby also involuntarily starts breathing through the nose right at birth, after floating in amniotic fluid for all his/her life. A chick does not have to be taught how to break the shell of the egg. A spider does not have to be taught how to spin a web. Right after hatching, without any help, instruction, or guidance, an Australian incubator bird (megapode) knows how to slowly dig its way out of the large temperature-controlled nest mound that its parent built to incubate the eggs. This process can take up to three days. A sea turtle instinctively makes its way to the water (and not the land) after it is hatched without any guidance from a parent. There are many such examples of things that baby creatures just automatically know right from birth without any instruction like what to eat or drink, who their predators are, and how to survive!

Bugs or Insects. Have you considered how beautiful and meaningful the process of metamorphosis is? How a caterpillar becomes a cocoon and turns into a beautiful butterfly? Have you observed the behavior of ants? How they work hard with each other as a team and how they identify each other and communicate through smell and touch? There is much we can learn from these creatures!

"Go to the ant, thou sluggard; consider her ways and be wise: Which having no guide, overseer, or ruler, Provideth her meat in the summer, and gathereth her food in the harvest" (Proverbs 6:6–8).

There are many other such interesting and amazing things to think about regarding the microorganisms and organisms that God has created. All this is not a coincidence or random chance! Through our study of the animal and plant world, we know that only those animals with better developed brains can perform complex functions. Therefore, we associate more complex functions with higher intelligence. Once again, I must emphasize that when we see complex functionality and brilliant "engineering," it is reasonable to conclude that an "Engineer" was behind all this. This "Engineer" deserves credit for His design and craftmanship!

BIOMIMICRY

Biomimicry is an area of engineering that studies and uses special design features observed in nature for engineering applications. Many inventions in the past have been inspired by design features observed in nature (e.g., Velcro, airplanes, etc.). As we have started figuring out how things work around us, we have been realizing that there is so much precision and ingenuity in the physical design and functioning of animals and plants in the natural world. So we have now started studying them very closely to see if there is anything we can adopt and mimic in how we design, build, and operate things in order to achieve similar results.

If man has taken thousands of years to reach a point where we could design, invent, and build the things we have today, a reasonably impartial thinker would hesitate to imagine that the great wonders and engineering we see in nature today just came into being somehow on their own without any intelligent external influence. The scientific world is deeply engrossed in studying the engineering marvels and design wonders in nature. Yet it finds great difficulty in acknowledging the hand of God in all these. Calling them "solutions that nature or life has found" is not really a scientific explanation that a logically minded person can be satisfied with. It can only be rationalized with the presupposition that it couldn't have been God, so what else was it?

Have you considered what the *driving force* could have been behind the brilliant and superbly engineered solutions that "nature has found"? Chance? Randomness? Is that really a scientific conclusion? Could it have been nature's laws? If so, how did the laws get established? And why are the laws permanent? Is it more aligned with the scientific approach (or just plain logical thinking) to say that "someone" did it or to say that "somehow some way" all this brilliance came into existence? Indeed, they who are well acquainted with the ways of God, the Maker of everything, will readily recognize His hand in all the ingenuity and excellence of design as the hidden layers are gradually exposed through man's study of science and nature.

A good example of biomimicry is the design of the Shinkansen bullet train.[15] The original design caused loud noise because of air pressure changes when emerging out of tunnels at high speeds. The design was modified, taking inspiration from the beak of a kingfisher, which smoothly dives into water with hardly any splashing. This resulted in improved efficiency and lesser noise.

Geckos' feet have very tiny hairs called setae that split into around a thousand branches each (approx. 200 nm in size). These create adhesive forces that, when combined, result in a force so strong that it can possibly lift around 250 lbs. Although the adhesive force is so strong, the gecko can detach its feet from the wall. This dry, clean, and reusable adhesive property is attractive to scientists for possibly manufacturing tape, climbing boots, etc. for numerous applications.

The spider's web is being studied at a molecular level to learn about and possibly mimic its great strength, light weight, and elasticity for commercial production. Spider's silk is five times stronger than Kevlar (used in bullet-proof jackets). Unlike Kevlar, which is made at high temperatures using petroleum products and sulfuric acid, it is made in the spider's body at body temperature and without any corrosive acids.

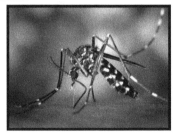

Mosquitos have a way of piercing our skin without our knowledge. Usually, we don't realize that a mosquito is biting us until it's too late! This happens because their mouths have several moving parts that pierce into the skin. Scientists are looking at the way the mosquito's mouth is designed to develop needles that pierce human skin painlessly.[16]

Lotus leaves have a water-repellent property. When a water droplet falls on this leaf, it rolls off without sticking to it or making the leaf wet. This is due to the presence of microscopic bumps on the leaf, specifically the nanoscaled tubes that stick out of the bumps. This nanotechnology is being studied for application in the clothing and paint industries.

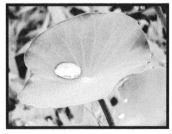

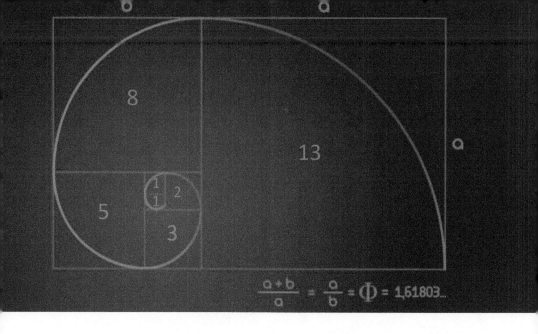

$$\frac{a+b}{a} = \frac{a}{b} = \Phi = 1{,}61803...$$

MATH IN NATURE

I personally find mathematics to be very interesting. Even the simple laws and theorems that we learn from our elementary through high school years are intriguing. Take the multiples of 9 for instance. From a young age, I have been amazed that the digits in all the multiples of 9 add up to 9 (1+8=9, 2+7=9, 3+6=9, etc.). In the same way, I find the Pythagorean theorem, the sum angle theorem, the laws of trigo-nometry, and many other mathematical theorems to be fascinating.

Fibonacci Series, Fibonacci Spiral, and the Golden Ratio

It is then more fascinating that God has embedded mathemati-cal phenomena in nature. The best example for this, in my opinion, is the Fibonacci series. This series of numbers starts with 0 and 1. Each subsequent number in the series is the sum of the previous two numbers (0+1=1, 1+1=2, 1+2=3, 2+3=5, and so on). The Fibonacci series is represented below.

0, 1, 1, 2, 3, 5, 8, 13, 21, 34, 55, 89, 144...

Using these numbers, the Fibonacci spiral is obtained by drawing circular arcs that connect the corners of squares that have the numbers in the Fibonacci series as the length of their sides placed next to each other.

The golden ratio (ϕ) is defined as the ratio of two quantities such that the ratio of their sum to the larger quantity is equal to the ratio of the larger to the smaller quantity. Its value is an irrational number (1.618033...). Consecutive numbers in the Fibonacci series approach the golden ratio (more so for higher numbers in the series).

We can observe many instances of the Fibonacci series, the Fibonacci spiral, and the golden ratio in nature. The number of petals in various flowers like lilies, daisies, buttercups, and the like follow the Fibonacci series. The way that the petals are arranged also follow the golden mean ratio (i.e., number per turn). This same number is seen in the seed head arrangement in flowers like the sunflower. Following the golden mean ratio number for this arrangement allows for a tight packing and maximum filling of the space without any gaps. This causes the seed heads to be arranged as spirals. The number of spirals formed by this arrangement also tends to be a number in the Fibonacci series. This spiral pattern can be seen in other plants, fruits, and vegetables like the pine cone, pineapples, strawberries, cauliflower, and the like.

The golden ratio can be seen in proportions for bodies of humans and animals. Some have also observed that the ratio of females to males in the colony of bees is typically the golden ratio. The Fibonacci spiral can also be seen in the design of shells, galaxies, hurricanes, and so forth. There are many more examples that I will not attempt to cover any further.

What was the "force" that drove the adoption of these numbers for design across various species? What motivated them toward order and perfection in their design (e.g., sunflower seed head arrangement)? Randomness again? Chance? Somehow, some way? Although the discovery of the series and the spiral can be credited to the Italian mathematician called Leonardo Bonacci, God had placed this unique sequence in His creations even before the Fibonacci series was discovered by humans!

Examples of Fibonacci numbers and spirals in nature. *Pineapples and pine cones have a double set of spirals running in clockwise and counterclockwise directions. The number of these spirals are found to be adjacent numbers in the Fibonacci series. Similarly, sunflowers have a spiral seed arrangement in the clockwise and counterclockwise directions. These spirals are also consecutive numbers in the Fibonacci series. This can be seen in other flowers as well (e.g., daisies). The number of petals in many flowers follow the Fibonacci series. For example, a daisy may have twenty-one or thirty-four petals. Other examples of this include lilies, buttercups, etc. The Fibonacci spiral is also found in the shape of spiral galaxies, nautilus shells, and snail shells.*

FRACTALS

Fractals are patterns that have smaller subunits of the same pattern in them (pattern within a pattern within a pattern, and so on). If we zoomed in on a fractal, we would see the same pattern at different resolutions. In the first two man-made patterns displayed on the next page, smaller units of a particular pattern are used to form larger patterns that look the same. Fractal patterns that are generated mathematically can be infinite. However, those that are observed in nature are finite due to obvious physical constraints.

For example, fractals are seen in geographical features like mountain terrain (mountains within mountains), branching of rivers, and so forth. Branching patterns seen in lightning and frost formation are some other examples. The way that trees branch out can be viewed as fractals as they have branches within branches within branches, and so on. My favorite fractal in nature is broccoli (or cauliflower), which has subunits that represent the larger bunch. A fern leaf looks like a leaf from afar, but upon close examination, it reveals leaves within leaves within leaves (i.e., each unit by itself looks like a leaf). I find fractal patterns to be just some more examples of fascinating design features that can be observed in nature and show God's wisdom and purposeful work in creation.

Some examples of fractals. The first two are artificially gen-erated, and the others are naturally occurring.

The Romanesco broccoli is a great example of a vegetable that has fractals _and_ the Fibonacci spiral.

The cheetah is specifically designed for high-speed running on land, with features like a small head, enlarged nostrils for more oxygen intake, a light-weight body, a large heart, bigger blood vessels to supply more oxygen, a flexible spine for spring-like flexion and extension, and a long tail for stability.

KINGDOM SECRETS

MYSTERIES OF THE
KINGDOM OF GOD

This book has focused mainly on understanding the things of God that are hidden in nature. There are also many mysteries about the *kingdom of God* that are revealed through the things that we see in the natural world. The Bible is filled with parables, "shadows," analogues, metaphors, and comparisons. God uses many of these in His loving and living "user's manual" to man in order to reveal much about His own nature, His will, plans, and His Kingdom. Since we are obviously constrained in our ability to understand and weigh spiritual and heavenly concepts through our senses due to our limited exposure to such things, He uses comparisons and analogies so that we can relate these to things we already know and have experience with.

For example, God compares His own relationship with us to many of the relations that we have on earth. Those who have received

God's salvation through Jesus Christ are called God's children (*"But as many as received him, to them gave he power to become the sons of God, even to them that believe on his name"* [John 1:12]). God is compared to a father who knows how to give good gifts to his children (Matthew 7:11). God also compares His pity toward us and His merciful, forgiving heart to that of a father (Psalms 103:13; Luke 11:13). He comforts His children like a mother (Isaiah 66:13). The relationship between Christ and the church is compared to that of a husband and wife (Ephesians 5:22–32). Jesus called His disciples friends and brethren (John 15:14: Matthew 12:49). We are referred to as God's servants (Matthew 10:24). There are a number of other human relationship analogies in the Bible that help define our relationship with God.

In the Bible, Christ is represented as an innocent, spotless Lamb that was offered as a sacrifice for us (John 1:29), a Good Shepherd who gave His life for His sheep (John 10:11), a Friend Who loved us greatly and laid down His life for us (John 15:13), the right Door for us to enter into (John 10:7), the Light of the world that lights everyone in darkness (John 1:9), the True Vine that nourishes the branches (John 15:1), the Way to eternal life (John 14:6), the Bread of life (John 6:35), the Sun of righteousness (Malachi 4:2), the King of kings (1 Timothy 6:15), and much more.

In order to help us understand who we are in Christ, the church of God is compared to a flock of sheep (John 10), a garden (Song of Songs 4:12), a building (1 Corinthians 3:9), a holy temple (Ephesians 2:19–22), a spiritual house, a royal priesthood, a holy nation (1 Peter 2), and so on. As individuals, we are compared to trees that bear good, bad, or no fruit and called the temple of God (1 Corinthians 3:16). The spirit of a man that is born again is compared to wind that can be heard but not seen (John 3:8). Our works on earth are compared to gold, silver, precious stones, wood, hay, and stubble that will be tried with fire (1 Corinthians 3: 12). The trying of our faith itself is said to be more precious than gold that is purified (1 Peter 1:7), and God is referred to as a refiner of gold and silver (Malachi 3:3).

The Word of God (the Bible) is compared to seeds that were sown by a sower (Luke 8:5–15). Some fell on the wayside, on rocks, among thorns, and on good ground. This analogy is used to describe how different people receive the Word of God and the things of God that are spoken to them. Only the seeds sown on good ground bear abundant fruit. In the same way, the receptiveness (or openness, preparedness, etc.) of the heart plays a great role in how effective God's Word is in someone's life. The Word of God is also referred to as fire and a hammer that break rocks into pieces (Jeremiah 23:29), a two-edged sword (Hebrews 4:12), honey (Psalms 119:103), milk (1 Peter 2:2), and water (Ephesians 5:26) to illustrate its specific qualities. Jesus uses the examples of the birds of the air that do not sow, reap, or gather in barns and the lilies of the field that do not toil or spin in order to teach us how well God takes care of His creation and us (Matthew 6:28–34). The kingdom of God is like a field that has hidden treasure and like a precious pearl of great price that was found. When a man discovered the field and a merchant found the pearl, they sold all they had to purchase them. The kingdom of God is also compared to a field in which good seed was sown, a net that was cast into the sea and caught different types of fishes, a grain of mustard seed that was sown and grew up to be a tree in which birds lodge in, leaven which a woman took and hid in three measures of meal till the whole was leavened, and so on (Matthew 13).

So we see that God has used the things that we see and experience in nature and in our daily lives as examples to teach us about His kingdom.

"I am the good shepherd: the good shepherd giveth his life for the sheep" (John 10:11).

THE TRUTH

Truth is like a mountain. It is not affected by anyone's attitude toward it. Whether people choose to admire its presence or ignore it...it remains unchanged..

THE PURSUIT OF TRUTH

There is a lot of diversity in this world. We are diverse in color, language, backgrounds, culture, tastes, and race. Most significantly, we are diverse in our beliefs. Our traditions, upbringing, education, experiences, and exposure have mainly shaped what we believe today. Most people are comfortable with their beliefs and usually reluctant to make significant or radical changes.

However, regardless of what anyone believes, the truth is a constant. If two people disagree on something (assuming their viewpoints are contrary to each other and the matter is not something subjective like taste or preference), usually there are only two possibilities—one person is wrong, or both persons are wrong. So for matters of great consequence, an unprejudiced pursuit of truth is very important. This usually requires a denial of self, a true humbling of the heart, and sometimes a willingness to suffer some losses.

Truth can be likened to a mountain in the midst of a city filled with busy people. Some people may choose to reject, ignore, or forget its presence. Some others may choose to marvel at it, scale it, or share pictures of it with others. No matter what anyone chooses to do with it, this mountain remains completely unaffected. It is completely independent of those who acknowledge or reject its presence. It existed even before the city existed and remains in its place, unmoved, unchanged, and true.

We know that the physical laws of nature were always true even before we discovered them. For instance, the earth has always been spherical, even when man believed that it was flat. At the time, perhaps all the world believed in the so-called fact that the earth is flat. Yet the truth of its spherical shape still remained as it were from the beginning. All truth—whether spiritual or physical—likewise remains unconditional and unchanged, detached completely from its seekers and followers (or non-followers).

Therefore, it is important to pursue the truth about God and spiritual matters without any prejudice, presumptions, or presup-

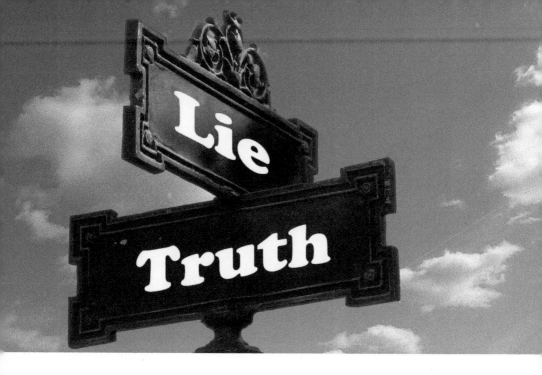

positions resulting from prior influences. Remember the questions about God that were presented at the beginning of this book? Add to those some more very important questions like the following:

Who is God?
Why should I seek this God?
Why should I change what I believe today?
What is the purpose of my life?
What happens after I die?
Is there any hope beyond the grave?
Is there anything to look forward to?
Can I know for sure? If so, how?
What is the consequence of ignorance?
Is there a judgment day?
If so, how can I escape God's judgment?

Regardless of what someone may already believe about God (whether it is that He exists or that He does not, or whether it is belief in a certain religion), I assume that anyone can agree that knowing the truth about the above questions is of utmost importance.

Do you remember any incident or circumstance in which someone has tricked you, or stolen from you, or deceived you, or fooled you (in a non-joking way)? Do you remember a time when you realized that you made a mistake? Do you remember an instance in which you lost something valuable? Do you remember how you felt when these happened? I do. It was not pleasant. A feeling of *helpless regret* is one way to describe it. My point is—no one likes to lose something valuable, make mistakes, be deceived, or believe something false. I can assure you with perfect certainty that helpless regret is guaranteed if we are mistaken on the truth about the above questions.

So I urge you toward a *diligent* and *sincere* pursuit of the truth regarding these matters. The burden lies upon each individual to seek the truth and to verify and validate their own beliefs impartially and confirm that they are not just blind traditions, false deductions, or mere untrue opinions. It may be easier and more comfortable to remain affixed to a certain viewpoint. But it is critical for each person's *own benefit* to search for the truth with an openness for correction and change, *especially in matters of great consequence*. You may wonder—what is at stake? How serious of a consequence are we talking about here? How must this search be done? All this is what I am attempting to explain in the next few pages.

FAITH

It is important to talk about faith when talking about the pursuit of truth. A common misunderstanding is that the application of faith is restricted to matters of religion. However, it is not easily recognized that faith is an integral part of every individual's intellectual development and character formation from a very young age. Indeed, faith plays a large role in establishing values, beliefs, opinions, and knowledge in every area, not just religious ones.

For purposes solely in relation to our current discussion, let us define *faith* simply as believing something that has not been personally tested, proven, or verified and adopting it for personal application on some level. With this definition in mind, I believe that all of us can easily acknowledge without much hesitation that right from our youngest days, we have put our faith in many people who have had some form of influence in our lives. We started with first putting faith in our parents or guardians and then expanded it to others like siblings, teachers, friends, role models, and so forth. We accepted the many things they taught us—in faith. This includes matters of religion, morals, values, common sense, practical living, science, and much more.

So in other words, our lives started in faith and progressed in faith. From the time we were babies, our physical, mental, and moral development has involved believing and trusting in the many people who led and influenced us. Later in life, we may have had opportunities to test and verify many of the things we learned. However, at the time, we hardly had the chance or ability to verify and validate their words, but we took initial steps of faith (knowingly or unknowingly, willingly or unwillingly).

We also put our faith in things written by people we have never met or known personally. Almost all of us almost automatically had faith in our school and university textbooks and curriculum and perhaps our education system in general. I am personally not familiar with any student who has challenged what was provided as facts, knowledge, or good information in their school or university classes. The integrity, assumptions, or methods of scientific research are commonly not challenged or personally verified by individuals. These are generally trusted as worth believing (this is not to imply that they are not worth believing, but I am only emphasizing the role of faith in our world).

Many people who reject the existence of God (despite the overwhelming evidence of His artistic touch, wisdom, and power displayed in the visible and invisible aspects of the natural world and the universe as a whole, as discussed throughout this book) do so based on their faith in the written works of many others.

So we can see that faith plays an unrecognized but important role in our lives today. In some way or the other, to some degree, even today we still continuously exercise faith in our everyday lives—in authors, columnists, scientists, engineers, researchers, religious leaders, politicians, professional experts, leaders, television personalities, activists, news reporters, friends, YouTubers, and other strangers on the internet—and to some extent allow them to influence what we believe and the values we hold without having the opportunity to directly, conclusively, and personally verify the veracity of their words. The reason for saying all this is to highlight that faith is not just limited to religious applications and that using faith to approach truth is not such a far-fetched or unreasonable idea. Without realizing it, we all have taken steps of faith to get where we are today. In the same way, pursuing the truth about God requires taking initial steps of faith.

Some people regard faith in God to be the result of superstitious influences. They may weigh it as an uninformed, blind belief in the unknown that resulted from inherited traditions or during a desperate search for supernatural interference to meet needs and desires or as explanations to life's many otherwise inexplicable mysteries (like extraordinary circumstances or coincidences). This turns out to be true if this faith is not rooted on a personal relationship with the true eternal living God, the Creator of the universe. Indeed, most religious pursuits are based on superstition or blind faith in traditional beliefs. This only reinforces the utmost importance for a quest for the truth about God, because ultimately, only the truth matters.

People practice Christianity in mainly two different ways: (1) as a religion and (2) as a relationship with God. Religion usually focuses on trying to please God through self-sacrifice, good works, enforcing rules and restrictions, and the like. However, the Bible says that the only way to please God is *through faith*! Christ has already sacrificed Himself. We do not need to earn our salvation through works. His work on the cross is sufficient to save us. Faith in God and His Word will produce good works as a fruit.

So what I am advocating is not really somewhat of a blind or superstitious sort of faith in a religion or a god or prophet or church or religious leader or religious sect. I am instead recommending the same kind of faith that was applied through the majority of learnings that we gained in our life as discussed above. Faith that will be proven, validated, and confirmed as truth. Faith that will be strengthened through evidence from real-life experiences and personal communication with the true living God. If you think about it, is that not the scientific approach? Let me explain what I mean.

THE SCIENTIFIC METHOD

Is it possible to know the true living God, the Creator, beyond any doubt? The answer is yes. *But how can this be done?* If we cannot see Him or interact with Him as with another human being, how can we know for sure that He exists and Who He is? One way is to apply the scientific method.

Science is simply a study of nature. All the different branches of science—physics, chemistry, biology, mathematics, and the like—involve a systematic approach to unraveling the truth (the deep hidden secrets) about nature, including the things that cannot be seen. To be consistent and to ensure that the results are credible, scientific study follows a method. Broadly speaking, there are three main steps in the scientific method. The first step is to make observations regarding the question that has been formulated. Based on these observations, reasonable hypotheses are formed, which is the second step. In the third step, these hypotheses are tested repeatedly and validated by experimentation before they are declared as believable results and established as laws, facts, or truths.

If I have not already done so, let me point out that neither science nor the true application of the scientific method contradicts faith in the true Almighty God and vice versa. One can remain a strong believer in God and still believe in and enjoy science (like I do) without compromising good reason and logic. The Bible—the book that reveals the true God and Creator of the universe—does not have to be followed blindly or enforced by any ecclesiastical authority. They who have verified it to be the truth follow it wholeheartedly without any coercion or enforcement.

The Bible

So if you have not already read it, you may be wondering—what is the Bible all about? What does it contain? Well, it contains historical events (starting from the creation of the earth and man), prophecies, poetry, teachings, instructions, warnings, promises, commandments, and even a few scientific facts (which were discovered

by man thousands of years after they were written in the Bible). It also reveals God's identity, greatness, power, wisdom, works, ways, thoughts, will, plans, goodness, mercy, compassion, care, sacrifice, love, and many other things. It also reveals God's relationship with man and what God has done for mankind when this relationship was compromised. It is not a set of rules and regulations that binds us to a certain religious form of life. It is the truth. It is a firm foundation that we can build our lives on without fear or doubt.

But how can one know for sure that the Bible is the truth? Well, other than studying the historical and archaeological evidence available to us regarding the people, nations, and events described in it and the many prophecies in it that have been and are being fulfilled, it's just a matter of using the scientific method on a personal level. That is, by following the steps of observation, development of hypotheses, and experimentation, one can verify the Bible and its revelation of God to be true, its contents to be worth accepting, its promises to be worth believing, its advice and guidance to be worth following, and so on. In this process, the experimentation step needs to be done in faith.

As discussed previously, faith is not absent in our general approach to science. For many of the things that we accept as facts and truth in general, only a few people are actually involved in the application of the scientific method. The majority of the world's population tends to believe what they read without personal verification, as long as it is presented in a textbook, scientific journal, magazine, newspaper, on the internet, and the like. This is probably due to the faith we have in the systems that are in place to regulate these. I am not implying here that these systems are not trustworthy. I am only highlighting that we trust them to a certain extent. The Bible, however, can always be tested by every individual, which is a better approach for verifying the truth. This privilege is not really available for many of the books and ideologies that are accepted as truth and presented as scientific fact.

Some people find certain parts of the Bible or certain concepts in it hard to understand, especially things about God and His identity as the Father, Son, and Holy Spirit (one God but three personalities). However, something being hard to understand does not imply that it is not true. For example, it is extremely difficult for a five-year-old child to understand trigonometry. This does not mean that there is anything wrong with trigonometry itself. It is just that the child has not matured enough to understand something as complex as trigonometry. He/she has to go through a systematic educational process involving many years of experience in mathematical concepts in order to develop the intellectual capacity to study trigonometry and other complex subjects. In the same manner, there may be many things about the Bible that may not seem to make sense initially, but these things become clearer and clearer as our walk with God progresses. Even when someone else tries to explain some things, it may still not make much sense at first. This happens because of a lack of spiritual maturity on our part and this gets better as we know God and grow in Him through a relationship with Him.

This has been my own personal experience. As my experience with the Bible progressed over the years, I have been able to understand more and more depths and mysteries hidden in its contents. This is true especially in the context of personal life applications. It can be compared to unearthing hidden treasures of great value. This is a very sweet and rewarding experience. So my personal interaction with Jesus Christ, the true eternal living God and Creator of the universe, through the reading and hearing of the Bible and through life's many experiences and circumstances have time and again (almost on a daily basis) reinforced and strengthened my faith as a Christian. This privilege is available to all individuals. So let us look at how the steps of the scientific method can be applied to understand the truth about the Bible and God.

Observation

There is much to observe about God in nature. An in-depth study and knowledge of science and the observations made regarding the natural world can provide great insights about the God Who created it. In fact, this book you are reading focuses largely on these observations in nature.

We can also "observe" many things about God through the experiences that others share about Him. Their accounts of their own personal relationship with Him, what they have heard and seen from Him, the answers to prayers they have received, the small and great miracles that they have experienced in their own lives, the guidance that they receive from Him, the blessings that they receive daily (e.g., hope, love, joy, peace, contentment, freedom, strength, etc., to name a few), and their testimonies on the manifestation of biblical truths in their lives can be treated as observations. These can be regarded as objective and untested observations as far as the unbeliever is concerned. To ignore these would be to forsake a sincere quest for truth.

The ultimate authoritative and comprehensive "book of observations" about God is the Bible. This book describes and details the ways, works, will, heart, nature, intentions, and plans of the true Almighty God. So an unbeliever can make many observations about God and other truths pertaining to life and eternity by simply reading from this book or by hearing someone else read it, explain it, expound it, or preach from it. These can remain as mere theoretical "observations" until they are personally tested and proven by faith.

Formation of Hypotheses

The conclusions that we form from all these several different types of observations mentioned above can be treated as hypotheses. For example, when we observe God's work in nature, we can reach conclusions about His attributes like His power, glory, wisdom, and love (as I have done in this book). When we hear from others about Him, we can reach conclusions regarding the reality of His existence, His ways, His unmatched and unconditional love for us, His mercy, His faithfulness, and His goodness. When we read the Bible or hear a sermon, we can form similar conclusions about God's goodness, will, plans for us and the world, great love, power, justice, judgment, mercy, and grace.

Experimentation

This is the step that establishes the hypotheses (or conclusions as described above) as facts or truth beyond doubt. So if done with an unbiased mind, these conclusions about God and the Bible that resulted from the various methods of observation described above can be tested and proven in one's own personal life by taking steps of faith.

Steps of faith

These steps of faith may require some self-denial or involve some uncomfortable and drastic changes to one's life, beliefs, and customs. For the sake of discovering the truth about someone so great as God, and for the sake of the possibility of having a close and loving relationship with Him, and when the consequence of being wrong or deceived is so great, these steps of faith, in my opinion, are absolutely worth the difficulties that may accompany them. One example for a step of faith that you would need to take for a relationship with God is prayer. By this, I do not mean that you will need to recite something from a prayer book or repeat words or sentences constructed by someone else. Instead, I mean an honest and open dialogue with God, believing that He is lovingly listening. I am talking about praying sincerely while expecting an answer! This can be a prayer uttered secretly in your mind; but it must be honest, sincere, and directed to the Almighty God. You may not know Who He is, but He certainly knows every thought and thirst in your heart. You may not hear from Him or receive an answer immediately, but if you are really seeking a revelation of the true God, persistent and sincere prayer to Him will certainly not go unanswered or wasted. Faith is needed to start praying and keep praying to the invisible God. As your relationship with God grows, your faith (or belief) only gets stronger and stronger.

"But without faith it is impossible to please him: for he that cometh to God must believe that he is, and that he is a rewarder of them that diligently seek him." (Hebrews 11:6)

Another step of faith is treating the Word of God (the Bible) as the truth, reading and studying it with an open and believing heart, and taking steps to follow its advice and guidance. The Bible describes itself as living, powerful, sweet, and nourishing. If you are able to take this step of faith in believing the Bible, you can certainly experience these qualities of the Word of God.

It is described as living because the way it interacts with you is similar to how a living person would. It accompanies you in your journey of life as a close companion. It always addresses your current state and speaks to your heart based on your current issues, thoughts, needs, and so forth. It provides timely guidance, comfort in sorrow, assurance in anxiety, deliverance from fear, answers for questions, and advice for decisions based on your current need and circumstances. As a source of light, it shows us the way and directs our feet in the path of righteousness and toward eternal life.

"Thy word is a lamp unto my feet and a light unto my path" (Psalms 119:105).

It is described as powerful because it can change the hardest of hearts and the most stubborn disbeliever. It can break the strongest chains of sin and work great miracles in your life through its application. It is described as sweet because of how it makes us feel often. The lives of the men and women described in it provide great encouragement and serve as good examples of what to do and what not to do. Usually the sweetness of God's Word (the Bible) is most experienced in times of difficulties. It is also compared to milk that provides nourishment to babies. It is the Word of God that helps us grow in our faith and in our relationship with God. Just like babies grow by drinking milk, our inner man grows through nourishment by the Word of God.

Other steps of faith you can take include listening to another person's testimony of their experiences in their relationship with God or explanation of biblical concepts, starting to attend Bible study gatherings and church services, asking questions and seeking answers from experienced Christians, and so forth.

Taste and see

The blessedness and joy of a true believer of the Bible is that each individual can maintain a personal relationship with God. And this relationship offers the opportunity to test, taste, and prove the goodness of God as described in the Bible. Just like in human relationships, as we draw closer to God and as our relationship with Him matures, we get to know His nature and many aspects of His personality better. To those who are interested, He reveals Himself and enables them to delight in Him. This God I am describing is truly awesome. The Bible says: *"O taste and see that the LORD is good; blessed is the man that trusteth in Him"* (Psalms 34:8).

Once, when I was shopping at a grocery store, I was hanging around some papayas, trying to decide whether to buy them or not. There was a couple in the vicinity of these papayas who were also contemplating the same matter. Interestingly, neither of the two had eaten a papaya before. So one of them asked me, "What does this taste like?" This proved to be a rather difficult question, and so I struggled to come up with an answer. In my mind, I could remember the taste of a papaya, but I had no words to describe it. So one of them asked, "Is it like a mango?" to which I replied, "Yes, sort of…in texture…but not in taste." I don't remember what I finally told them, but I do remember thinking they just need to buy and eat one to find out how it tastes. The point of mentioning this incident here is that you just have to taste some things to know what it's like.

Christian life is a little like the example of the papayas. You will not fully understand its sweetness until you taste it yourself. You can hear about it, read about it, or others may describe what they have experienced. But to taste the goodness of God yourself is some-thing else. Through your life experiences, when you personally hear from Him and when you experience His gentleness, His company in loneliness, His assurance in uncertainty, His strength in weakness, His courage in fear, His help in difficulties, His wise guidance, His abundant grace and mercy when you fail, His care and protection, His love that surpasses human logic and judgment, the peace that He promises when you are troubled and anxious, and much more through your relationship with Him, your faith gets strengthened day by day and you grow in your understanding of Him.

The Holy Spirit

A wonderful promise that Jesus gave to His followers is that He will be with them always, even until the end of the world. Although His physical presence is not here with us now, Jesus promised that He will dwell within us if we truly love Him and keep His words. This happens through the dwelling of the Holy Spirit within us. Can you imagine anything more wonderful than having the Spirit of the Almighty, Most Holy, and Great God dwelling within us? To put this in perspective, consider that even a meeting with your company CEO is not an easy everyday thing. A world leader (like a ruler or president) is a much harder possibility. Although the "important" personalities in this world are so inaccessible due to their limitations and practical constraints, the Creator of the universe is not only accessible and avail-able to listen to us at any time and any place, but He has also promised to dwell within us by putting His Spirit within us. Indeed, I can truly witness that the constant presence, communion, and guidance of the

Holy Spirit is an amazing thing to experience. I cannot forget the day that God unexpectedly filled me with His Spirit and how I felt. It was a great and bright power that filled me during a prayer meeting. None of the people around me or my own family knew what happened, but the immense joy that filled me was wonderful!

Divine influence and revelation

As Christians, we can also witness firsthand many instances of God's divine influence, presence, and provision. We come across many humanly inexplicable circumstances and turn of events in our life. Some refer to these as miracles.

For example, answer to prayer is a privilege that Christians experience on a regular basis. Whether the petition be small or great, it is not a coincidence that we receive answers from our loving heavenly Father. Sometimes, even small desires that spring up in our hearts are heard and answered by God. I have many personal experiences in which specific prayers were answered and requests were granted, both for myself and for others. These experiences keep building my faith in God and in the power and effectiveness of prayer to Him. I have also heard many testimonies from other Christians about how God answered their prayers. Even just recently, I heard from my uncle about how God provided an immediate answer to his prayer right after he rose up from prayer that day. He had specifically asked God to give him an answer that same day, and God miraculously granted His request just as he finished praying. These kinds of experiences are common, and they glorify God's name greatly among His believers and fill our hearts with amazement and gratitude toward Him.

Answer to prayer is a great faith-strengthener. Answered prayer reinforces the truth for God's children that there is indeed a God in heaven Who knows us, cares for us, and hears our silent thoughts directed to Him. It solidifies the fact for us that our prayer is a conversation with our heavenly Father. So we do not just superstitiously and blindly utter prayers that we have memorized or read to an unknown being in the hope that "someone somewhere" is listening. A true Christian can pray with confidence and faith that his/her prayers are being heard.

However, prayer is not like the wishing wells or magic lamps that we read about in fables. It is not a means of fulfilling all our wishes and dreams. So every desire and want that we express to God does not necessarily get granted. Prayer is just an act of communicating with God. He is able to do anything, and there is nothing impossible for Him. However, He is good and does what He wills. So we can always pray with the confidence that He is listening. But He mercifully and with the wisdom of a Father grants what is best for us at the right time according to His will.

God revealing the future through dreams, visions, and prophecy is another significant faith-strengthener. We read of many instances in the Bible where God has revealed something to man through dreams and visions. Sometimes, these dreams and visions needed to be interpreted to understand what they mean. For example, the dream seen by the Pharaoh of Egypt about a future famine was only understood after Joseph interpreted it. In some cases, they provided guidance to the one seeing it. For example, the Apostle Paul saw a dream about a Macedonian man asking him to come and help them. This dream inspired him to travel to that region to preach about Jesus.

My wife and I have both seen dreams and visions about future events that have been and are being fulfilled (amazingly, some which included specific names of people!). This is not something uncommon among Christians. In fact, many people have seen visions of Jesus in their dreams (especially in Arab countries where the chance for exposure to the Bible or Christianity is very limited).

History has shown many biblical prophecies for the world being fulfilled. Many are being fulfilled even now. I have experienced prophecies about my own personal life (i.e., God speaking specifically to me through other people) being fulfilled. Also, there have been countless situations where God has spoken to me and very appropriately addressed the current and relevant circumstances of my personal life (my fears, anxieties, worries, complaints, needs, sorrows, etc.). This happened through sermons from the Word of God (unbeknownst to the preacher) or a reminder and explanation of the practical application of biblical text in my heart during my personal prayer time. As a confirmation of God's message to me, there have been countless instances where I have heard the same Bible verse quoted or the same things being said or preached on the same day or in the same week by two (and sometimes more) different sources completely independent of and unknown to each other. On many occasions, I have heard hymns and songs being sung in church services that God gave in my heart earlier the same day.

Although I have attempted to highlight above how the truth about God and the Bible is reinforced through our personal experiences as Christians, I must emphasize the need for some caution regarding relying solely on experiences (even seemingly "supernatural" ones) for determining truth. It is not too hard for the human mind to be deceived. Illusionists succeed by this very principle! Supernatural occurrences should never be the foundation of our faith. A Christian's experiences with God reveal His nature. They are a result of his relationship with God and help in the development of this relationship. It is dangerous to superstitiously seek and rely on supernatural experiences and manifestations without a strong and sound personal relation with God and a good knowledge of the Bible.

Also, there are several professed Christian ministers and televangelists who attempt to display miracles and healings in the name of Jesus for personal gain and fame. These are not to be confused as works of God. They are usually tricks employed by these deceivers for beguiling the masses. There are many false prophets who use the name of Jesus and false prophecies to deceive many people. The devil has also been known to show signs and wonders to deceive many people. However, miracles, dreams, visions, and experiences that occur from a personal relationship with Jesus only reinforce the truth in what ought to be the real foundation, the Bible.

Freedom

Freedom from the bondage of sin is one of the biggest miracles that God performs in the life of His children. Personal freedom is commonly misunderstood as just having the ability to freely pursue our desires and objectives and do what we want without any restrictions, especially religious ones. Being submissive to God's commandments may have the appearance of an unpleasant and limiting lifestyle. In reality, this is not the case in the life of a true follower of Jesus Christ. Firstly, God never forces any of us into a relationship with Him or into obedience of His commandments. He may allow some circumstances and bring some people into our lives for us to hear about Him and know Him. But He gives us the freedom to make our own choices.

He has shown us the way to eternal life. He has also informed us about the way to eternal damnation. Both of these are well documented in the Bible. However, He doesn't push any of us onto any of these paths. He may influence us through events in our life and interaction with others. However, He ultimately gives us the liberty of making the choice for ourselves. Starting from Adam and Eve, the first man and woman in the garden of Eden, man always has been given the freedom to choose whether to believe God and keep His commandments or not. However, having the freedom to choose does not necessarily guarantee that we will make wise choices that result in good consequences. That is why it is a good choice to believe God and submit to His authority. A child growing under the authority of his or her parents may feel restricted and robbed of freedom (especially in their teenage years when they foolishly think that they are already wise enough to make decisions on their own for their lives). However, their restricted life and subjection to parental authority usually guarantee protection from error (and associated consequences) and future benefits that they may only realize after many years.

Even in worldly political, corporate, and social systems, leadership and authority play vital roles in the success and failure of those systems. We see that laws, codes, rules, and regulations are commonly seen as necessary to define boundaries, regulate conduct, and punish offenders. This helps to maintain order within these systems and facilitate progress. God's leadership is better than any other leadership this world has ever seen in any realm. He is righteous, just, wise, loving, and abundantly merciful. Even though God is supreme and deserves honor and worship from every created being simply because He is God, He does not enforce His authority in a dictator-like or tyrannical way. He is often compared to a loving Father and a caring Shepherd in the Bible. Anyone who willingly chooses to subject themselves to His authority and walk according to His commandments will only find themselves rejoicing along their life journey. It becomes burdensome only when religious rules and regulations are established and followed based on man-made religious systems and principles (including seemingly Christian ones) separate from a personal relationship with God Himself.

Jesus Christ told us that the way to destruction and eternal suffering is very broad, and there are many on that road. The broad way generally represents the popular and easy way. It is not a surprise then that the majority of the world rejects God's plan for man's salvation and is headed to eternal damnation. However, the way to eternal life is narrow. This implies that Christian life is not meant to be about prosperity and comfort in our life here on earth, as some portray it. It may involve losses, sacrifice, self-denial, suffering, persecution, and pain. However, it leads to eternal joy, peace, and life with Jesus Christ, and that is what should matter.

So for an outsider, the life of a true Christian might seem restrictive since his life journey is on the narrow way. However, if you pay close attention to the details, you can see that the Christian's life on the narrow way is filled with a lot of hope, joy, peace, contentment, and freedom. Nonetheless, it is true that blind religious practices often associated with self-imposed restrictions and constraints in the hope of pleasing God or performing "good works to counter the bad" are unpleasant, worthless, and unnecessary.

Although there is a perceived sense of freedom when you do not subject yourself to God's commandments and authority, this is not true freedom at all. Sin actually robs us of true freedom since it ultimately leads us to everlasting torment that cannot be escaped from. The Bible says that the sting of death is sin. This means that if our sin is left uncleansed by the blood of Jesus and if we are not justified before God by our faith in Jesus, death is an absolutely terrifying thing to face. This, in no way, resembles anything close to freedom, and I highly recommend that you consider this very seriously.

Freedom from sin (and from God's judgment due to it) is truly a marvelous thing and sweet to the soul. I can truly testify that there is great joy associated with the assurance of forgiveness and acceptance by God. Sin of any form only works to enslave its clients. The nature of sin is that it lures with empty promises as it first did with Eve, the first woman. The only forbidden fruit in the garden of Eden was good to look at, seemed good to taste, and she thought that it would make her as wise as God. These qualities of the fruit from the tree of knowledge of good and evil that enticed Eve represent the three forms of temptation that still work in the world today to draw us away from God—the lust of the eyes, the lust of the flesh, and the pride of life (1 John 2:16). So the fruit looked appealing to Eve and seemed like it had something to offer beyond what God had provided in the rest of the garden and all of earth. She did not believe God's word that she would die if she ate it. So she exercised her God-given freedom to choose and elected to believe the serpent. We know by now that her choice in disbelieving God was the biggest tragedy in human history. Death, pain, suffering, sickness, and all human toil and trouble entered this world due to Adam and Eve's poor choice. So although sin offers to quench the desires of our hearts and thirsts of our souls, it ultimately fails to provide anything that lasts long or satisfies our true needs. Sin may provide a temporary relief for our longing, but we find no permanent fulfillment or contentment by its indulgences.

This is why many people struggle with various forms of addictions like drugs, alcohol, cigarettes, tobacco, food, gambling, pornography, sexual desires, social media, video games, movies, love of money, love of possessions, craving for attention, or even harmful, draining, and demanding premarital or extramarital relationships. Usually, people tend to indulge in these things due to an underlying thirst in their hearts. However, anyone who has experience with an addiction will confess that indulgence never thoroughly satisfies. The longing and the thirst for more springs up quickly, no matter how much you indulge. For some people, the thirst keeps growing, and the addiction escalates to stronger forms. It blinds their morals and leads them to irrational actions. It causes them to do things that they would not normally allow themselves to do (e.g., lying, deception, stealing, etc.). It takes away peace from their hearts and leads to depression. It binds, imprisons, and restricts their personality and hinders them from functioning up to their true potential. It affects their relationship with those who love them (spouses, parents, siblings, friends, etc.) and hurts them deeply. It affects their performance at work or at school, and they find opportunities for success vanish right in front of their eyes because of their addiction(s). They find their money drain out without control. For extreme addicts, life becomes all about satisfying their craving, and everything else loses priority. If any of these things resembles your life even remotely, let me assure you that there is hope in Christ, our Deliverer.

Whether you are an addict, or a "casual sinner," no one in this world can deliver you from the bondage and power of your sinful lusts like God can. We can attain freedom from even the most addictive and enslaving sins by His power. I am not referring to a long, painful, drawn-out rehabilitative process but a quick, easy, and relieving deliverance from the clutches of repetitive and self-destructive habits and actions. In fact, God's work usually results in a lack of interest and sometimes even a repulsion toward things that once used to draw us like moths to a fireball. Those who have experienced this will no doubt confess that this work of God is nothing short of a miracle. Indeed, many hardened hearts have been softened by His love, and many who were captive to their addictions have been freed by Him. This can only be possible through God's love and power.

Once, while talking to a Samaritan woman who was known to be living in sin, Jesus said, *"But whosoever drinketh of the water that I shall give him shall never thirst,"* (John 4:14). Later, He proclaimed the same truth to the crowd at a Jewish feast saying, *"If any man thirst, let him come unto me, and drink."* (John 7:37). He is not talking about His ability to provide an endless supply of H_2O here. His invitation and promise here is to quench the deep thirst(s) in our soul—for love, fulfillment, success, acceptance, entertainment, pleasure, and the like. Jesus also said,

Come unto me, all ye that labor and are heavy laden, and I will give you rest" (Matthew 11:28).

He has promised to remove the weight of sin and give us eternal rest if we are willing to approach Him in faith.

Undoubtedly, the biggest miracle that God has wrought in my own life is the changes He has brought in my own character and the victories He has been giving me in my personal battles. I cannot yet claim that all has been conquered, but He has delivered me from so many things that weighed down on my conscience like great, unremovable burdens.

I am amazed at the way He has so lovingly and gently pointed out flaws in my character that no one else could. Most often, we tend to explain away or justify our own shortcomings. If someone was to point something out about our character, we tend to take a defensive stance. Self-pity is a commonly used defense tactic that helps us build a rather impenetrable wall around us. When we pity ourselves (sometimes even with unrelated things that happened to us), we tend to justify ourselves and prevent ourselves from judging (or examining) ourselves impartially. In this state of mind, what is really right or wrong loses relevance. We take a victim stance that is quite damaging for our own selves. The Bible says, *"Who can understand his errors? cleanse thou me from secret faults"* (Psalms 19:12).

This Bible verse implies that it is not natural for anyone to understand their own errors. However, it is in our best interest to understand our own mistakes. An approach that usually works great is to step outside of our self-justifying perspective and try to see things from God's perspective. This is not easy during times of conflict and disagreements, but I have found this to be quite rewarding!

Another defense mechanism we have is to try to project the person pointing out our error, flaw, or shortcoming as a hypocrite and therefore render him/her unworthy to say anything about us (i.e., trying to find a way in which the faultfinder has failed in that same area or some other). Another defense strategy that we employ is blaming others or our circumstances for the things we say or the way we behave. In these ways, we unknowingly build forts around ourselves so that our own conscience is protected from being stirred or impacted in any way. However, it is beneficial for us to let our pride take a fall so that we can correct our errors and be built into someone better.

The Bible compares God to a potter and us to vessels shaped by Him (Jeremiah 18:2–6). It also says that we are God's workmanship (Ephesians 2:10). So like a carpenter builds furniture, God intentionally and methodically builds us into something that He designed and purposed in His mind, provided we allow Him to do so. I am very grateful to God for the ways in which He allowed my times of failures, difficulties, conflicts, pain, and sorrows to show me the truth about who I am and the areas in which I need to change. Although this is not an easy process, I have been able to realize through much self-examination that the problem is not just with my outward behavior but lies deeply embedded in my character, that is, the person that I am. As Jesus said, a good tree cannot bear bad fruit, and a bad tree cannot bear good fruit. The problem, therefore, is with the tree itself. The fruits (my behavior, words, actions, etc.) that I was/am bearing only revealed what kind of a "tree" I am.

Our character is a result of a mixture of many things that affect us—our inborn nature, our experiences starting from childhood, the people and things that influence us, and so forth. Only God can really make a bad "tree" good. This change that God brings in us is not limited to a mere giving up of bad habits or an increase in religious activities. It addresses the depth of our individual nature, our motives, our desires, our character, our integrity, and other such things that influence our direction, priorities, goals, actions, words, and thoughts. The Bible says that when a person becomes a Christian, a new man is created in him. So the change that happens in us is not just in what we do but more importantly in who we are and why we do things.

No amount of piety or religious works can make us good. But God can miraculously change our evil hearts into one that mirrors His goodness. The Bible says that we are being changed from glory to glory until we become conformed to the image of Jesus (2 Corinthians 3:16–18). I am thankful to God for the ways in which He has been changing me, my attitude, my approach, my perspective, my direction, my priorities, my goals, and the like over the years that I have known Him and walked with Him. I am so grateful to Him for picking me up every time I fall, fail, wander away, and disappoint Him. I am indebted to Him for His unending mercy, the hope that He preserves in me, and for the assurance of His love and fatherhood that He gives me during those times. God never leaves nor forsakes His children, regardless of how far they have drifted away from Him.

To illustrate this, Jesus once narrated the parable of a son who asked his father for his share of the inheritance. His father granted his younger son's request and divided his wealth among his two sons. Not many days later, the son took his share and left his father's house to pursue a life of pleasure and self-indulgence (Luke 15:11–32). To me, he seems like a person who knew what he wanted in life and pursued it. Or in other words, he exercised his freedom to choose, and his father honored his choice. After a while, when all his money was exhausted due to his extravagance and pursuit of pleasure, he found himself in a condition so pathetic that he would often desire to fill his belly with a portion from the pigs' food, but he could not. Finally, he decided to return to his father with a plan to request him to hire him as one of his servants.

When he drew near, his father saw him from a distance. He had compassion on him and ran to meet him. He embraced him and kissed him. He then told his servants to clothe him with the best robe. He had them put a ring on his hand and shoes on his feet. He then arranged to celebrate the return of his son with a feast. God is like the father described in this parable. Even when we think that we have exhausted all possible mercy from Him, He is compassionate and always ready to receive us. So if your guilt and shame are keeping you from approaching Him, be assured that He will receive you into His house with open arms. This is why the Bible says,

"O give thanks unto the LORD; for he is good: for his mercy endureth for ever" (Psalms 136:1).

I am not saying this just based on what the Bible says but also on how this has been real and true in my own personal life.

New life in Christ

Jesus once attended a wedding in a place called Cana (John 2:1–11). When there was a shortage of wine at the feast, He asked his disciples to fill up the waterpots with water and serve to the guests. They obeyed and served the water, and it miraculously turned into wine. When the ruler of the feast tasted the new wine that Jesus made, he was greatly impressed. He did not know that Jesus had made the wine from plain water. He commented to the bridegroom that usually people serve the good wine at the beginning, but he has reserved the good wine for now. The new wine that Jesus made is symbolic of the new life that He gives. You may be content in your current state of ignorance and separation from Him, but you will only realize what you are missing when you have tasted this new life for yourself. It has purpose, meaning, and hope beyond the grave.

In another place, Jesus said that no one who has drunk old wine will desire the new wine because he will say that the old is better (Luke 5:39). The old wine represents the pleasures of life in this world. A person living in sin and pursuing pleasure, prosperity, and leisure in this life does not easily understand the bliss or value of the new life that Jesus gives through a relationship with Him. There is no natural desire or inclination toward this new life. This may be your state right now. You may not feel the need or see the benefit of pursuing a relationship with Jesus. You may be indifferent about it or greatly opposed to the idea. However, Jesus promised us abundant life in Him. You will only understand its value and experience the great joy, peace, and relief it gives when you personally taste of this new and abundant life—here on earth and in eternity.

Jesus used some parables to describe the blessedness of the kingdom of heaven. In one such parable, He said that the kingdom of heaven can be compared to treasure that was hidden in a field (Matthew 13:44). When a man found this treasure, he joyfully went and sold all that he had and bought the field. He also compared the kingdom of heaven to the example of a merchant man seeking good pearls (Matthew 13:45–46). When he found one pearl of great price, he sold everything he had and bought the pearl. In both these parables, Jesus has highlighted the great value of attaining eternal treasures through faith in Him. The value of this is much greater than everything that you may have to suffer or sacrifice for the sake of accepting the truth.

This is why many people throughout history have suffered great losses for the sake of accepting the truth of the gospel of Jesus Christ. During the first century AD, when the apostles of Christ started spreading the good news of God's salvation for all men by faith in Jesus, the Jewish religious leaders started persecuting them. They imprisoned some of them and killed some of them. Stephen and James the apostle are among the first who were killed. This caused the believers of Jesus living in Jerusalem during that time to flee (and hence to take the gospel to other parts of the world). That is how Christianity initially spread. However, Christians later started experiencing persecution at the hands of the Roman empire. Throughout history, we can see that many of the true followers of Christ were apprehended, questioned, threatened, imprisoned, beaten, tortured, and killed for their reluctance to forsake their commitment to Christ and for their attempts to share the good news of this valuable gift with others. This still happens in many parts of the world even today in modern times, especially in countries with limited religious freedom.

Growing up in a Christian home, I have personally heard testimonies of people from my own native place who had lost wealth and suffered poverty and hunger for the sake of following the truth of the gospel of Christ. Some had been treated as outcasts or suffered abuse and torture at the hands of family members and their society. My own paternal grandmother was beaten by my grandfather with a stick and forced back home from the river where she was just about to take baptism. He also managed to shove the pastor who was about to baptize her. However, God changed my grandfather's heart that same week, and he joined her at the river to take baptism the following week.

Throughout history, many Christians have endured hardships due to the way of truth they have chosen to follow. These ordinary men and women chose to suffer these things and refused to deny Christ (some of them even at gunpoint or at the point of execution) for two main reasons: (1) they realized that the value of what they had attained in Jesus far surpassed any losses they had to suffer in this life (including their own lives) and (2) what they have believed (i.e., the Bible) is the truth. Dying for the truth was worthwhile for them.

WHAT LIES BEYOND?

There is one truth that none of us can deny or escape. Our life on earth must end. This weak, mortal, and corruptible body that is prone to decay must one day be laid in the grave. As discussed earlier, we have made tremendous advancements in research, technology, and science. Yet none of our inventions or discoveries have ever been able to prevent death. Perhaps delay, but never prevent. This is the boundary that God has set for our life on earth—everyone must die.

No matter who we are or what we have achieved in life, we must leave behind our bodies, achievements, wealth, possessions, positions, friends, family, hobbies, careers, and so forth and succumb to this truth that awaits all of mankind. All the great men and women that history boasts of—kings, emperors, tyrants, dictators, warriors, political leaders, scientists, artists, scholars, philosophers, sports personalities, movie stars, musicians, celebrities—all have bowed down and surrendered before this "grave" reality, and so must we.

So with this in mind, there are some important questions we can/should ask:

1. *What lies beyond the grave? Although there are several theories and opinions surrounding this, what is the truth? After all, it is only the truth that matters.*
2. *What can we do to be best prepared for this truth? What is the point of all our toil, pursuits, and passions in our life on earth? How can we reprioritize our goals and objectives in life based on this truth?*

The next few pages will address these important questions.

The Judgment

As noted above, there is no controversy regarding the truth that all of mankind is destined for the grave one way or the other. Some die young, and some die old, but all die. Beyond this, there is the judgment.

"And as it is appointed unto men once to die, but after this the judgment" (Hebrews 9:27).

"And I saw a great white throne, and him that sat on it, from whose face the earth and the heaven fled away; and there was found no place for them. And I saw the dead, small and great, stand before God; and the books were opened: and another book was opened, which is the book of life: and the dead were judged out of those things which were written in the books, according to their works… And whosoever was not found written in the book of life was cast into the lake of fire" (Revelation 20:11–12,15).

After we spend our limited time here on earth, we must all appear before God to receive His judgment on how we will spend eternity. No one can escape this nor stand and justify himself/herself before the righteous and just God Who knows and sees everything.

Some people describe the prospect of hell as unfairness or cruelty on God's part. I have heard the commonly asked question, "Why would a loving God send people to hell?" To understand this, all we need to do is think about our worldly system of laws and justice. When

an offender or lawbreaker is apprehended and punished, we normally say that "justice has been served." Hardly anyone would condemn a jury or judge for convicting and sentencing a murderer or rapist. In fact, we would be upset and frustrated if someone known to break the law is let go scot-free. Not only do victims seek justice, but even people who are completely unassociated with the crime desire to see offenders punished. That is one reason why some court trials are attended or closely followed on the news by people unrelated to the case.

Recently, a nation celebrated the execution of four men convicted for their group assault of a young college girl. The torture inflicted on the girl that ultimately led to her death was a horrible incident that shocked the entire nation. So when those men received the reward for their deeds from the nation's judicial system, it was not a surprise that there was no sign of complaint from anyone. Instead, many rejoiced and felt that she was avenged. In another recent case in a different nation, a young father was convicted and sentenced to several years in prison for his role in the death of his four-year-old daughter. In this case also, there were many who were outraged because of the incident (especially due to the fragility and innocence of the victim) and expressed their relief and satisfaction in the conviction and sentencing of this man.

In both these cases and all other cases, you will notice that justice is perceived as a good thing (by law-abiding citizens, not criminals). Punishment for offenders is desired and never condemned as unfair. In fact, many would tend to consider mercy or pardon as being unfair, especially in cases of extreme crimes. So then why is it so hard to understand God's justice and judgment? Why do we need to frown when He is only maintaining the justice that is expected of a fair judge?

God executes judgment based on His laws. They are like the laws of nature—unchanging. Our opinions on what is fair, good, or right do not define what is right in His eyes. He cannot and does not show partiality. So if you are guilty, you must be punished because that is how justice is served in His court.

The Good News

Yet by now, we know that this is not the entire story. The truth does not end with the news of the judgment. We are all sinners and have in some way or the other violated His laws. A criminal cannot undo his/her crimes in front of an earthly judge through acts of kindness, service, or good will. Similarly, we cannot justify ourselves before God with any good works that we do. We have come short of God's supreme standards for righteousness and are guilty before Him. There is nothing we ourselves can do to repay the great debt of sin upon us or remove its heavy burden. The weight and guilt of sin always remains on us. We can never prove ourselves to be innocent before Him because of our inherently sinful nature that is perpetually prone to error. *Yet God has not left us to merely spend our days on earth fearfully awaiting the revelation of His wrath and judgment.* He has not left us without hope or a way for a deliverance from the torment of hell and the lake of fire. He is too great and His love toward us is too deep to allow that. Although we deserve punishment, God has done something *extreme* to justify us and save us from this.

Because of His deep and unmatched love for us, He decided to bear the weight and guilt of *our* sins on Himself. Being the Almighty God, He left His glory in heaven, humbled Himself greatly, and took on the form of a weak and mortal man, His creation. Jesus did this to reconcile us to God and bridge the great gap we have with Him due to our sins. He lived righteously on earth, performed great miracles, and fulfilled the will of God, the Father. He lived as though He had nothing and eventually suffered oppression and affliction at the hands of the men He created. Jesus was mocked, reproached, spat upon, and tortured. He willingly suffered the pain and shame of dying on a cross in order to save us from the guilt, shame, and consequence of sin. He was innocent, but He died like a criminal so that we may be justified before God. However, He defeated death and resurrected on the third day with a glorious, incorruptible, and immortal body. He ascended to heaven after this and now intercedes on behalf of all who believe in Him. Through Him we have forgiveness from God, victory from the bondage of sin, hope, joy, peace, and eternal life.

"But he was wounded for our transgressions, he was bruised for our iniquities: the chastisement of our peace was upon him; and with his stripes we are healed. All we like sheep have gone astray; we have turned every one to his own way; and the LORD hath laid on him the iniquity of us all" (Isaiah 53:5–6).

"And if any man sin, we have an advocate with the Father, Jesus Christ the righteous: And he is the propitiation for our sins: and not for ours only, but for the sins of the whole world" (1 John 2:1–2).

If we *believe* in Jesus's sacrificial death on the cross for our sins, we can stand before God's judgment seat completely justified and free of guilt. Jesus acts as an advocate (or defense lawyer) on our behalf in order to justify us before God, the Father. God will pardon every sin small and great in our life if we accept His way of salvation for us. This is not because of our righteousness or goodness, but because of Jesus's righteousness and His sacrifice. This is the best gift you will ever receive in your life—a way to escape eternal damnation and enter into eternal life through Jesus's death on the cross for you. The value of this gift is immeasurable.

Jesus said,

*"I am the good shepherd: the good shepherd giveth his life for the sheep…*and *I lay down my life for the sheep"* (John 10:11, 15).

We also read in the Bible: *"For when we were yet without strength, in due time Christ died for the ungodly. For scarcely for a righteous man will one die: yet peradventure for a good man some would even dare to die. But God commendeth his love toward us, in that, while we were yet sinners, Christ died for us. Much more then, being now justified by his blood, we shall be saved from wrath through him"* (Romans 5:6–9).

Christ did not lay down His life for us because of any good thing we have done. Neither do we receive forgiveness for "becoming good." We can never meet God's standard of goodness on our own. The Bible says that while we were yet without strength and while we were yet sinners, Christ died for us because of God's love for us. It is not even common for someone to die for a good man. Who will die for a sinner? Imagine someone volunteering to take on the guilt and punishment for one of the four men executed in the assault case described earlier. It is not just the severity of the punishment (i.e., death by hanging) that makes this an impossible scenario. Who will feel like doing anything good for such vile men who heartlessly inflicted so much violence on that defenseless girl? Dying in their place may seem like a ridiculous idea that no normal person would feel like doing. Yet this is exactly what Jesus has done. The Bible says that when we were considered the enemies of God, He reconciled us to Himself by the death of His Son, Jesus. Even the vilest, most offensive, heartless, ruthless, hardened sinners can receive forgiveness and pardon through the blood of Jesus, including the four who were executed (if they chose to receive it while they were alive).

"Come now, and let us reason together, saith the LORD: <u>though your sins be as scarlet, they shall be as white as snow;</u> though they be red like crimson, they shall be as wool" (Isaiah 1:18).

Usually, if someone sacrifices something for another person, it is seen as a good thing. If a man risks his own life to save someone else's, he is called a hero. He may be honored with an award or medal depending on the circumstances. The person whose life was saved would most likely feel hugely indebted to the rescuer. However, for some reason, Christ's sacrificial death for all of mankind is not only undervalued but also mocked and despised. The name of Jesus is the most blasphemed name ever. We see it being misused in books, television shows, movies, social media, and surprisingly even in the news. Why is this so? Is it fair that His name and good deed for us is made fun of? Why is His name used as a curse word? What is it about the exemplary life He led, the great miracles He performed, the good things He taught, or the sacrifice He went through for all humanity that is worthy of hatred, reproach, rejection, scorn, or ridicule?

If a criminal was to receive pardon from a worldly court system, it would be considered extremely foolish of them to reject it. For example, if someone sentenced to life in prison receives an early release after serving a couple of years, it would not be normal for them to choose to ignore this and remain incarcerated. This pardon extended by the court would typically be welcomed and received with open arms. However, surprisingly, many people willingly reject the way of salvation and pardon from God's judgment. It is not God's will that we spend eternity in hell. The Bible says that hell was originally made for the devil and his angels (Matthew 25:41). The loving God of this universe gave nothing short of His own self so that we may escape the just punishment for our sins. But if we refuse to accept God's way of salvation through faith in Jesus, His just sentence will stand. The reasons why people shun God's mercy are many, but the consequence is the same.

The Severity of Consequences

A lot of people underestimate the severity of eternity in hell. I have heard people casually comment that they are ready to go to hell.

Some people thoughtlessly say, "to hell with it" or "go to hell." It is obvious that they have no idea what they are talking about! So to present a clearer picture, here's a summary of what to expect.

Everlasting torment

Our time on earth may hardly be eighty or ninety years. Although this may seem long to some, it is no comparison to eternity, which is an infinite period of time. Comparing our life here to eternity is like comparing a tiny speck of dust to the infinite expanse of the universe. If pain and suffering are hard to bear here on earth, how would torment be tolerable for an unending period? This is a serious thing to think about. To assess your tolerance level for pain, think of a time when you were in pain due to an illness or injury (or even a simple kick on the shin or stubbing of the toe!). To understand what the lake of fire may feel like, imagine a time when you burned a part of your body! The horror of an eternity in hell is too often ignored or underestimated!

Separation from God

Banishment to the lake of fire also means separation from the presence of God. Today you may not realize how God's provision and mercy has been preserving you even though you may not acknowledge Him or believe in Him. It would be a devastating and painful experience to be separated from God's presence for an infinite period. It is hard to imagine how desperate that condition would be because it means that one can never experience the warmth of God's loving company ever again. Today we know our company with God gives us peace, comfort, and joy. Imagine how blessed it would to be with Him forever and how heartbreaking it would be to be separated from Him forever.

Regret

Have you ever looked back on a mistake you have made or a good opportunity you have let go? Have you ever wished you could go back and change a situation or how you acted in that situation? I have plenty of examples from my own life experiences.

Regret is a very difficult feeling to experience and is almost always associated with a feeling of helplessness. The regret in hell will be unbearable for all those who have refused such an easy way offered by God for them to escape it. It is a sad and terrible mistake to forsake God's mercy and *free gift* of salvation through Jesus Christ. Hindsight may be twenty-twenty, but it is completely useless in this case! Foresight and appropriate action are what is needed.

Shame

There is a lot of shame associated with sin. That is probably why some people who have been arrested for a crime hide their faces from the cameras. Even a child caught red-handed in an act of disobedience or naughtiness displays shame! Adam and Eve had no shame about their nakedness before they sinned. Yet the minute sin entered their lives, they were ashamed. There is coming a day that we will stand naked before God like Adam and Eve did. That is, our true nature, works, words, intentions, and so forth will be displayed openly as we stand before Him. God is our Creator, and He knows everything about everyone inside out. The only covering for our shame due to our uncleanness and filth is Jesus Christ's blood and His righteousness. So standing before God's judgment throne can be a very shame-filled experience for you if you have not already confessed your sins to Him openly and received forgiveness and cleansing through the blood of Jesus.

"Neither is there any creature that is not manifest in his sight: but all things are naked and opened unto the eyes of him <u>with whom we have to do</u>" (Hebrews 4:13).

"And many of them that sleep in the dust of the earth shall awake, some to everlasting life, and some to shame and everlasting contempt" (Daniel 12:2).

Hopelessness

Whenever we experience a difficult situation, sorrow, or loss in our lives, a hope for a better tomorrow does great things to lift our spirits and drive us forward to face the next moments, days, and years ahead of us. An expectation that the current "storm" will pass and things will get better empowers us to face troubles bravely. Having something to look forward to helps us move forward. There is never a hope for a better tomorrow in hell. "This too shall pass" is not a statement anyone can make about any of the suffering in hell. Things will never get better, and there is nothing to look forward to. This is such a horrible thing to experience! For this reason, I urge you to make the best of the opportunity you have today and not to overlook God's pardon through faith in Jesus!

So we see from the above summary of consequences that there is a lot at stake, and the consequences are huge. How we spend our lives on earth—what we choose to believe, our values, our objectives, our goals, the choices we make, the way that we follow, how we live—will determine how we are to be for an unending period. If we are mistaken in our beliefs and opinions, we have a lot to lose. Oh, how diligent we must be in seeking and following the way of truth!

Denying the Truth

There are many people who dismiss or deny the truth about God's final judgment. There are some who are ignorant of it and many who refuse to accept it. However, as with all truth, it is irrelevant whether some accept it or reject it. Imagine an accused in a crime trying to defend himself in court by saying, "I do not agree with this law!" or "I do not accept this law!" or "I did not know it was against the law!" The law is the law, and the judge does not care whether an individual agrees with it or accepts it. He will be tried and sentenced based on the law regardless of whether he likes it or knew it or agrees with it or not.

The laws of God are in fact like the laws of nature. They do not change with the passage of time or based on any man's interpre-

tation or personal opinion. They are truth. They are unchanging. No man can disannul, disqualify, or dispute them. He set them, and He is the judge because He is God. He will examine, and He will proclaim the sentence. When someone drives a car, the burden lies upon the driver to learn the traffic laws and abide by them. In the same way, *the burden lies upon every man to know what God's laws are and how he can abide by them.* To further illustrate the concept of ignoring or rejecting laws, consider the following hypothetical scenario:

Suppose there was a man who loved skydiving and went up to jump from a plane. He makes the jump along with others. After having fallen a certain distance, another man notices that this person has jumped without a parachute! So he quickly shouts across to him mid-drop, "Friend! Where is your parachute?" to which he responds, "Oh, I don't need one."

Astonished, the second man asks him, "What do you mean?"

"Well, I think this free fall is great fun! I want to continue this way all the way down. The parachute reduces the thrill and excitement of the fall," he replies.

Now, the second man's amazement grows as do his eyes, "But without a parachute, you're going to hit the ground and die!"

"Oh, I don't believe in that."

"What do you mean you don't believe in that? It's basic science! When you go up to a great height in the plane, you build up a lot of potential energy. When you jump, the law of conservation of energy comes into effect, and this potential energy gets converted to kinetic energy. This means your velocity increases greatly until all the potential energy will have been converted to kinetic energy. By the time you hit the ground, your velocity would have reached its maximum. This results in your hitting the ground with a great force. Since your body is not built strong enough to withstand this force, your eventual demise is inevitable!"

Hearing all this, the man responds cheerfully, "Oh, I don't believe in all these laws of science! They are just a result of someone's imagination. So I don't think any of that will happen to me."

Now, this scenario and conversation may sound absurd and really far-fetched. It is. I was just trying to make a point with this extremely unrealistic conversation. Does this person's belief or unbelief have any effect on the laws that govern nature (e.g., the laws of gravity and conservation of energy)? Absolutely not! They are not dependent on anyone's opinion, knowledge, or lack thereof. They are truth. So we can imagine the consequences that such a person will face because he did not believe in the truth. Tragic, right? It is the same with the laws of God.

Are You Guilty?

So the question is, what will happen when you face the judgment seat? Will God find you guilty? Do you think you will enter into eternal life or eternal shame after your death? Do you think you will be cast into the lake of fire? Is your name written in the Book of Life (Revelation 20:15)?

Your natural inclination may be to think, "I think I am a fairly good person. Surely, God will accept me into heaven despite all the errors and shortcomings in my life!" But our standards for goodness or innocence are not necessarily right.

The Bible offers some foresight regarding all these.

"That they are all under sin. As it is written, <u>There is none righteous, no, not one</u>:... For all have sinned, and come short of the glory of God" (Romans 3:9–10, 23).

There is no one in this world who can claim that they are born righteous or sinless. David the Psalmist says in Psalms 51:5 that he was in sin from the time of conception: *"Behold, I was shapen in iniquity; and in sin did my mother conceive me."*

Sin has led all of mankind astray, and so we all fall short of God's standards for holiness and righteousness. In addition to this, the "works of the flesh" make you guilty in God's eyes and prevent you from inheriting eternal life.

"Now the works of the flesh are manifest, which are these; Adultery, fornication, uncleanness, lasciviousness, Idolatry, witchcraft, hatred, variance, emulations, wrath, strife, seditions, heresies, Envyings, murders, drunkenness, revellings, and such like: of the which I tell you before, as I have also told you in time past, that they which do such things shall not inherit the kingdom of God" (Galatians 5:19–21).

"Know ye not that the unrighteous shall not inherit the kingdom of God? Be not deceived: neither fornicators, nor idolaters, nor adulterers, nor effeminate, nor abusers of themselves with mankind, Nor thieves, nor covetous, nor drunkards, nor revilers, nor extortioners, shall inherit the kingdom of God" (1 Corinthians 6:9–10).

"But the fearful, and unbelieving, and the abominable, and murderers, and whoremongers, and sorcerers, and idolaters, and all liars, shall have their part in the lake which burneth with fire and brimstone" (Revelation 21:8).

Some people consider some sins or works of the flesh more serious than others. So as a result, their indignation may be voiced or displayed against certain types of sins, but they may completely overlook or fail to acknowledge the gravity of some others. However, God views these trespasses against His laws with an impartial perspective.

Do you think you have committed any of these things in your life? We can see here that it is not in any way easy or even possible to meet God's standard for innocence. This is why we all desperately need a Savior!

"Thanks be unto God for his unspeakable gift" (2 Corinthians 9:15).

WHAT MUST YOU DO?

Suppose you want to go to a certain city, but the only bus that takes you there is old and rickety. However, there are plenty of deluxe buses available from that same bus station to take you to other cities far away from where you need to go. Would you hop on one of the good, comfy buses because you prefer a smooth ride? I hope your answer is no.

In this context, it is ultimately the destination that matters. A broad and smooth way does not guarantee that you will reach a good destination. Similarly, a narrow and rocky road is worth traveling on if it leads you to the right destination. The destination that you will reach is determined by the way you choose, that is, the choices that you make in life. You cannot go north on I-5 from San Francisco and somehow expect to reach Los Angeles. Many people sadly (choose to) remain ignorant about their direction in life with the expectation that somehow ultimately everything will turn out to be all right. This is a false expectation. It is imperative and in each of our own best interest that we make the right choices in life so that we can ultimately reach a good destination.

There are two destinations that we can reach at the end of our journey of life—eternal life or eternal damnation. As discussed earlier, Christ has already done the work for our salvation. That is why He uttered the words, "*It is finished*" (*John 19:30*) just before He died on the cross. *He has paid the full price, and there remains no more sacrifice or good works that are needed from our part for our cleansing.* There is no need for self-torture or pilgrimage. Yet in order for us to benefit from the finished work of Christ, we must believe the gospel and, as a result, make certain choices (take certain paths) in our lives. As a result of the faith and love we have for the One Who died for us, we must accept and live by the values and guidance prescribed in the Bible. The following are a few of the steps we must be sure to take to receive this free gift of salvation through Christ, begin our Christian life, and grow in our relationship with the Lord.

Being Born Again

"*Jesus said, "Verily, verily, I say unto thee, Except a man be born again, he cannot see the kingdom of God*" (John 3:3).

It seems like Jesus is laying out an unusual condition for entrance into the kingdom of God. How can someone be born again? Nicodemus, the person to whom Jesus is speaking here, was also confused. He asks, so then should a man go back into his mother's womb? Jesus was not referring to a physical rebirth. He was referring to a rebirth that happens in our spirit—*a.k.a. our inner man*. It is a work of God's Holy Spirit that happens when we start believing in Christ and obey His commandment to be baptized. The Bible says that when we are "in Christ," we become a new creation; that is, a new man is created in us. This is a miraculous spiritual work done by God, not by us. This new man cannot be seen by our eyes, but his existence becomes apparent by the change that happens in our life.

Believing in Jesus

"And they said, believe on the Lord Jesus Christ, and thou shalt be saved, and thy house" (Acts 16:31).

"That if thou shalt confess with thy mouth the Lord Jesus, and shalt believe with thine heart that God hath raised him from the dead, thou shalt be saved" (Romans 10:9).

The first step to attaining salvation through Jesus Christ is to believe in Him with all our hearts. This may seem difficult at first, but it becomes easier when we take steps of faith. Believing in Jesus practically means believing

1. that He is the Creator and Almighty God,
2. that He came down from heaven having left His glory and majesty and lived as a man,
3. that He was sinless,
4. that He suffered for our sins and died on the cross,
5. that He was resurrected on the third day with a glorious and immortal body,
6. that faith in His sacrifice is sufficient for us to receive mercy and forgiveness from God and for us to be wholly justified before Him,
7. that we escape the severity of everlasting fire because we are counted righteous because of our faith in Him, and
8. that He is coming again to gather those that believe in Him and live in sincere expectation of His coming so that they may live with Him as His people for all of eternity.

Believing in Jesus grants us the privilege of being the children of God. There is a subtle difference between believing and having faith. The Bible says that the devils also believe in God and tremble. Having faith (according to the Bible) means that our actions, desires, choices, direction, and the like are determined by what we believe. So believing in Jesus with all our hearts also means that we follow all that He has said, that we allow Him (His words and teachings) to change our lives, and that we strive to align our choices, our decisions, our values, our priorities, and our goals with the way that Jesus has shown. It would also mean to accept the Bible as our foundation for truth and to build our lives on the truth that it declares, as it is the Word of God.

Repentance

"Then Peter said unto them, Repent, and be baptized every one of you in the name of Jesus Christ for the remission of sins, and ye shall receive the gift of the Holy Ghost" (Acts 2:38).

"If we confess our sins, he is faithful and just to forgive us our sins, and to cleanse us from all unrighteousness" (1 John 1:9).

The first step to repentance is a realization that we are sinners. We tend to justify our own selves based on the standards of goodness and justice that are established by society or based on the standards that we determine for ourselves (e.g., good works, doing some things that are right, etc.). As discussed earlier, this would not work in a worldly court system. Our personal justifications for violating the law do not matter. So it certainly will not work in the heavenly court system where God is the supreme judge. To understand where we truly stand, we must compare ourselves with the right standard, that is, God's Word (the Bible).

To repent means to acknowledge and confess our sins, shortcomings, and inadequacies to God. It means to be truly sorrowful in our hearts about them and to turn away from them. It means to approach Him with a humble heart. It means to accept our helplessness and inability to justify our own selves and to turn to Him for mercy. When we confess our sins to God in this manner and ask Him to cleanse us and justify us by the blood of Jesus Christ that was sacrificially shed for us in our stead, He will forgive us wholly and count us as pure and righteous. This reveals how abundantly merciful and compassionate God is. No matter how great our sins are, the Bible says that we can be wholly cleansed. He will remove all uncleanness from our hearts and make us new.

"He that covereth his sins shall not prosper: but whoso confesseth and forsaketh them shall have mercy" (Proverbs 28:13).

Baptism

"Know ye not, that so many of us as were baptized into Jesus Christ were baptized into his death? Therefore, we are buried with him by baptism into death: that like as Christ was raised up from the dead by the glory of the Father, even so we also should walk in newness of life" (Romans 6:3–4).

To avail of the salvation that Christ has provided for us through His death on the cross and His resurrection from death, we must partake in these with Him by representing these through baptism. Baptism symbolizes the burial of the sinful "old" man and the resurrection of a "new" man who walks in the newness of life. This shows the change that happens in us and compares it to the death and resurrection of Jesus Christ. The newly resurrected man now no longer serves sin but follows and yields to God.

"For as many of you as have been baptized into Christ have put on Christ" (Galatians 3:27).

Fellowship

God gives much importance to the fellowship we have with each other as we become Christians. When God adopts us into His family, we start identifying ourselves as brothers and sisters in Christ. Just like a parent enjoys the love shared among their children, God takes great delight in the love and communion we share with each other. This fellowship has many benefits. It is an important and necessary part of Christian life. It gives us opportunities for sharing God's love and growing in our relationship with the Lord. As we share our life experiences and learnings from the Bible with each other, we can encourage and strengthen each other. That is why we gather for church services every week. The main objectives are to have fellowship with each other, pray together, sing and praise God together, and to hear and learn from the Bible together. Oftentimes, when we are weak, discouraged, uncertain, or anxious, we can gain new strength, joy, hope, and direction through our fellowship with others. God works and speaks through others. This is a constant and ongoing experience in my own life.

The Bible gives several metaphorical references to describe the church such as a building, a garden, a flock of sheep, a nation, a priesthood, and so forth. One such metaphor used is the church being the "body of Christ" and Christ being the "head." The people in the global church of Jesus Christ (regardless of denominational or organizational differences) are referred to as parts (or members) of this body. This is to highlight that we may look different and have different functions, but we are connected to the same "head" that directs us.

"For we, being many, are one body in Christ, and every one members one of another" (Romans 12:5)

"But speaking the truth in love, may grow up into him in all things, which is the head, even Christ: From whom the whole body fitly joined together and compacted by that which every joint supplieth, according to the effectual working in the measure of every part, maketh increase of the body unto the edifying of itself in love" (Ephesians 4:15–16).

Love is an integral part of this body. This love enables unity among the members in the body. God's intent is that through our fellowship with each other (and with God), we grow in character and represent the character of Christ more and more each day.

WHAT DO WE GAIN?

So what exactly do we gain from being a Christian? What do we achieve from having a relationship with Jesus Christ, the Creator of the universe? Well, we have discussed many things already. So the following is just a summary/recap of a few of the benefits of Christian life.

Peace with God

"Therefore being justified by faith, <u>we have peace with God</u> through our Lord Jesus Christ" (Romans 5:1).

"For if, <u>when we were enemies</u>, we were reconciled to God by the death of his Son, much more, being reconciled, we shall be saved by his life. And not only so, but we also joy in God through our Lord Jesus Christ, by whom we have now received the atonement" (Romans 5: 10–11).

In addition to the clemency that we obtain from God with regards to our crimes against Him and the release from the sentence of eternal damnation that we deserve, we also enjoy the benefit of having peace with God. The Bible says that we are considered enemies of God when we remain uncleansed from our sin. It is rather terrifying to have God as your enemy. It is certainly not an advisable state to be in. The work of Christ for us has brought us the peace we enjoy with Him. We are changed from being God's enemies to being His friends. *"Ye are my friends, if ye do whatsoever I command you"* (John 15:14).

Eternal Life with Christ

"For the wages of sin is death; but the gift of God is eternal life through Jesus Christ our Lord" (Romans 6:23).

"For God so loved the world, that he gave his only begotten Son, that whosoever believeth in him should not perish, but have everlasting life" (John 3:16).

As we have extensively discussed previously, eternal torment awaits all those who reject God and choose to continue in sin. However, there is much to gain for all those who believe in Jesus Christ, the Son of God, the true Savior of the world. God has provided us the gift of eternal life through Jesus. The toil and turns of life on earth take a toll on us. If things do not go well, our days seem long, burden too heavy, and life without hope. Eternity lasts forever. Imagine spending so long a time—either in the lake that burns with fire and brimstone, in the outer darkness where there is weeping and gnashing of teeth or in the pleasant and joyous company of Jesus Christ and many other saints and angels. The gift of eternal life is of great value.

Adoption as Children of God

"But as many as received him, to them gave he power to become the sons of God, even to them that believe on his name" (John 1:12).

This book has focused largely on highlighting the character and personality of God the Creator, particularly His greatness, power, and wisdom. To even be acknowledged by such a great person is a privilege by itself. Imagine the greatest king on earth knowing our name or allowing us the pleasure of his company. Christ is greater than every king who ever lived. He is indeed the King of kings and Lord of lords. To add to the gap between us and God due to His greatness and our smallness, sin had estranged us from Him and created a great rift in our relationship with Him. Filthy, corrupt, and unclean men do not match well with a righteous and holy God. Yet God loved us and made it repeatedly and persistently obvious that He wants a loving relationship with us—not as King and subjects, not as Commander and soldiers, not as Dictator and people but as Father and children. What in this world would prevent us from coveting such a great privilege?

This Father-child relationship with God comes with a lot of benefits. It is much better than any parent-child relationship we have seen on earth. God cares for His children. He takes responsibility for our present and future well-being. We can live with the assurance that we are safe and secure in His loving hands. He provides comfort in sorrow, direction for decisions, help in distress and difficulties, chastening and correction for errors, and much, much more. There is also the added advantage that He sees us and knows everything about us (unlike any human parent). With Him, there is never any misunderstanding.

"Like as a father pitieth his children, so the LORD pitieth them that fear him" (Psalms 103:13).

The Holy Spirit

"And I will pray the Father, and he shall give you another Comforter, that he may abide with you for ever; Even the Spirit of truth; whom the world cannot receive, because it seeth him not, neither knoweth him: but ye know him; for he dwelleth with you, and shall be in you" (John 14:16–17).

Those who are justified by the blood of Christ are given the promise that the Spirit of God will dwell in them. This may seem slightly confusing or hard to understand. Rest assured, it is a blessed and wonderful experience. We humans are by nature weak, unworthy, wretched, and unclean mortals. What a privilege it is then that the Spirit of the Almighty God would abide in us! The Bible says that our bodies become the temple of God where His Spirit dwells.

"Know ye not that ye are the temple of God, and that the Spirit of God dwelleth in you" (1 Corinthians 3:16)?

The Holy Spirit shows us what is right and wrong, teaches us from the Word of God, intercedes for us when we pray, and reveals to us the deep mysteries of God.

"But the Comforter, which is the Holy Ghost, whom the Father will send in my name, he shall teach you all things, and bring all things to your remembrance, whatsoever I have said unto you" (John 14: 26).

"Howbeit when he, the Spirit of truth, is come, he will guide you into all truth" (John 16:13).

"Likewise the Spirit also helpeth our infirmities: for we know not what we should pray for as we ought: but the Spirit itself maketh intercession for us with groanings which cannot be uttered" (Romans 8:26).

"But God hath revealed them unto us by His Spirit: for the Spirit searcheth all things, yea, the deep things of God" (1 Corinthians 2:10).

A Clear Conscience

"In whom we have redemption through his blood, even the forgiveness of sins" (Colossians 1:14).

Living with guilt is very difficult, especially when the consequences are severe. A life of faith in Christ gives us the blessing of a clear conscience before God. A guilt-free conscience is of great value, especially before God the Righteous Judge. The assurance of God's forgiveness is impressed upon our hearts as the blood of Christ washes away our sins when we believe in Him.

"And the blood of Jesus Christ his Son cleanseth us from all sin" (1 John 1:7).

"Blessed is he whose transgression is forgiven, whose sin is covered. Blessed is the man unto whom the Lord imputeth not iniquity, and in whose spirit is no guile" (Psalms 32:1–2).

"I acknowledged my sin unto thee, and mine iniquity have I not hid. I said, I will confess my transgressions unto the LORD; and thou forgavest the iniquity of my sin" (Psalms 32:5).

There is no sin too great, no stain too dark that He will not cleanse. That is the value of the precious blood that Jesus shed on the cross.

"There is therefore now no condemnation to them which are in Christ Jesus, who walk not after the flesh, but after the Spirit" (Romans 8:1).

Freedom from Captivity

"But now being <u>made free from sin</u>, and become servants to God, ye have your fruit unto holiness, and the end everlasting life" (Romans 6:22)

As we discussed earlier, our relationship with God enables us to take victory over the chains of sin that easily enslave us. These chains range from bad habits to addictive and self-destructive sins.

No one in this world can give us such quick and effective relief and respite from the tyranny of sin. God, through His power, delivers us and gives us a life of freedom.

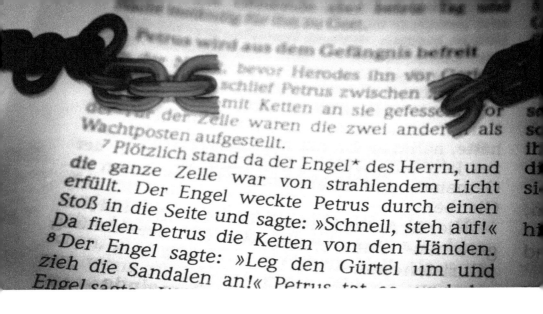

Love

The love that we receive and experience from people have limitations. Usually, it is conditional and based on expectations. It may change with time. However, *God's love is unconditional and unchanging*. Being able to understand and experience this love is a great blessing that Christians enjoy.

Friend, even if you are not a Christian, *God still loves you*. You do not have to fulfill His expectations or meet His criteria to be eligible to receive this limitless love. We discussed earlier that Jesus Christ died for us while we were still sinners. His love is better than any love you can receive from this world. You may have experienced disappointments in your life because you did not receive love from the people that you expected it from. You may even feel that no one really loves you. Friend, let me assure you that Jesus loves you deeply. His love can make up for any void or longing in your heart. His love provides contentment and comfort. He gave nothing short of His own life to save you from a horrible fate. I sincerely hope that you will receive this love and not reject it.

Throughout this section in this book, we have talked about many benefits of Christian life. There are probably many other blessings that may not have been covered here. Christian life is truly a joy and a blessing. We are blessed to be walking in close fellowship with

God and to receive His love. He manifests the evidence of His love each day in the way He leads us and fills our lives with joy, peace, and hope.

YOU MATTER

Do I matter to anyone? This question is being asked and becoming more and more relevant in today's generation than any other. That's why likes, views, comments, and subscribers on social media platforms are valued so highly (other than the monetary benefits, of course). Does anyone care about my opinion? Does anyone agree with me? Does anyone care about my life? Does anyone find me attractive? Does anyone care about what I do? Does anyone like me? Does anyone appreciate me? Does anyone love me? Truth is, nothing that is done on social media can fulfill our need for the assurance and privilege of being truly loved by someone else. Media platforms and worldly achievements may provide a temporary relief for our soul's longing but never a lasting one. History has shown us so many popular movie stars, musicians, sports personalities, and other people who are regarded as successful suffering from loneliness and depression. Their fame and wealth could not quench the need for their soul. Some have committed suicide, and others take refuge in harmful addictions and wasteful lifestyles. I have been surprised to learn that so many young people today suffer from mental health issues like depression, anxiety, and the like.

What is the biggest evidence that you matter to someone? Sacrifice, in my opinion. If someone sacrifices something to fulfill a need for you, it is reasonable to conclude that you matter to them. If a rich man gives you a small portion of his money, it is only a small indication that he cares about your well-being. But if he sacrifices most (or all) of his possessions for you, it is a good indication that you matter a lot to him. What if someone sacrifices their life for you? For instance, your life was in danger, but someone gave up their own life to rescue you from that danger. Would that convince you that you matter to them? That is exactly what Jesus Christ has done. His sacrifice on the cross is good and sufficient evidence that you matter to Him. Not just your physical, mental, emotional, or financial well-being while you're living in this world but also your eternal well-being after you depart from here. In fact, it is His deep and unmatched love for you that led Him to do this. What I am trying to convey here is that you can be fully assured that your thoughts, your beliefs, your joy, your wellness, your eternal future, and many more things about you matter to the God that created you—a lot. He wants you to draw near to Him and experience this love and care in your life. I have. I can assure you that it is wonderful.

CONCLUSION

So dear reader, what will you decide today? The evidence has been provided, the choice is before you, the consequences are huge, and the truth will not change. So here are some relevant questions to ponder upon: What do you perceive as the purpose for your life? In other words, what do you live for? What achievements in life can give you lasting fulfillment? What hope do you have beyond the grave? How sure are you of what you believe in today? What are you willing to risk for the sake of your traditions, beliefs, and opinions? How much of your life, future, and blessedness are you willing to place into the hands of those people (family, friends, teachers, politicians, authors, etc.) who have influenced you to believe what you believe today? What are the consequences of being wrong? What is the probability of you being wrong about something? Have you been wrong about something before?

If we weigh the severity of the consequences associated with this matter and the likelihood of error, it should not be hard to perceive that the risk is great.

May God give you the grace to know Him and turn your heart to the truth!

TOPIC INDEX

NOTES

1. www.space.com/25303-how-many-galaxies-are-in-the-universe.html
2. www.skyandtelescope.com/astronomy-resources/how-many-stars-are-there/
3. nssdc.gsfc.nasa.gov/planetary/factsheet/earthfact.html
4. www.universetoday.com/66647/how-much-bigger-is-jupiter-than-earth/
5. http://hyperphysics.phy-astr.gsu.edu/hbase/Solar/solflare.html
6. www.space.com/17001-how-big-is-the-sun-size-of-the-sun.html
7. www.universetoday.com/65356/how-many-earths-can-fit-in-the-sun/
8. www.space.com/17137-how-hot-is-the-sun.html
9. www.universetoday.com/13507/what-is-the-biggest-star-in-the-universe/
10. www.universetoday.com/106062/what-is-the-milky-way-2/
11. www.space.com/19222-largest-spiral-galaxy-universe.html
12. iupac.org/what-we-do/periodic-table-of-elements/
13. www.sciencedaily.com/releases/2011/08/110823180459.htm
14. www.youtube.com/watch?v=dECE7285GxU, Secret Megalopolis of Ants Uncovered—Truly a Wonder of the World!
15. https://biomimicry.org/biomimicry-examples/
16. Ibid

LIST OF ILLUSTRATIONS

All images are from www.pixabay.com.

223

(Dendrobates Tinctorius 'Azureus'); Water Melon; Blue Devil Damselfish; Capsicum; Paracanthurus Hepatus commonly known as Blue Tang; Robin Eggs; Pumpkin; Symphysodon commonly known as Discus Fish; Blackberries

8. *Page 24* Peacock
9. *Page 25* Bluejay
10. *Page 27* Lovebird; Cardinal bird; Weaver bird; Toucan; Zebra Finch; Magpie; Lorikeet; Scarlet macaw (Ara Macao); Hummingbird; Red Avadavat; Golden Pheasant; Flamingo
11. *Page 33* Dahlia; Daffodil; Bluebell; Vinca; Rose; Primrose; Tulip; Daisy; Poppy; Morning Glory; Jasmine; Purple Aster; Daisy; Columbine; Cornflower; Yellow rose; Gerbera; Hepatica; Orchid; Hydrangea; Pansy; Petunias; Water Lily; Tulip
12. *Page 38* Carolina Wood Duck
13. *Page 39* Puffins, Cheetahs; Grey Crowned Crane; Butterfly
14. *Page 44* Sombrero Galaxy (NGC 4594/M104)
15. *Page 51* NGC 3314 A/B overlapping galaxies
16. *Page 52* Vienna (Austria)
17. *Page 53* Rio De Janeiro (Brasil)
18. *Page 54, Page 55* Earth
19. *Page 56, Page 57* The Solar System
20. *Page 58 & Page 59* Jupiter and Earth
21. *Page 60, Page 61* Sun
22. *Page 63* Sirius Star
23. *Page 64* Andromeda Galaxy
24. *Page 65* Milky Way Galaxy
25. *Page 130* Termite mound
26. *Page 132* Cuttle fish; Stick Insect; Frog; Grasshopper; Weaver bird; Bacteria; Silkworm Cocoons; Skunk; Bees making honey; Beaver's dam; Ants communicating; Compound eyes of a Dragon Fly; Mantis shrimp
27. *Page 143* Romanesco broccoli
28. *Page 148* Cochin fishing

ABOUT THE AUTHOR

The author is an engineer who loves and enjoys learning about science and nature. He writes from the perspective of an observer who is fascinated by the beauty, diversity, and ingenuity found in nature. He uses his basic knowledge of science and fundamental engineering principles to describe the complexity in our created universe and to reach reasonable conclusions about these observations. He finds it a great treasure to have known the true living God and to have received the assurance of His salvation. He has written this book as a means to share this treasure with many others, especially his friends and family.

Printed in the USA
CPSIA information can be obtained
at www.ICGtesting.com
JSHW011609281023
50969JS00002B/2